Penguin Specials fill a gap. Written by some of today's most exciting and insightful writers, they are short enough to be read in a single sitting – when you're stuck on a train; in your lunch hour; between dinner and bedtime. Specials can provide a thought-provoking opinion, a primer to bring you up to date, or a striking piece of fiction. They are concise, original and affordable.

To browse digital and print Penguin Specials titles, please refer to **penguin.com.au/penguinspecials**

LOWY INSTITUTE

The Lowy Institute is an independent, nonpartisan international policy think tank. The Institute provides high-quality research and distinctive perspectives on the issues and trends shaping Australia's role in the world. The Lowy Institute Papers are peer-reviewed essays and research papers on key international issues affecting Australia and the world.

LOWY INSTITUTE

Inflection Point

A LOWY INSTITUTE PAPER

THOMAS WRIGHT

PENGUIN BOOKS

UK | USA | Canada | Ireland | Australia
India | New Zealand | South Africa | China

Penguin Books is part of the Penguin Random House group of companies whose addresses can be found at global.penguinrandomhouse.com.

First published by Penguin Books, 2026

Cover images by Eric Baradat via Getty Images (Biden) and
Nicholas Kamm via Getty Images (Trump)
Cover design by Ian Bruce, Lowy Institute © Penguin Random House Australia Pty Ltd
Typeset by Midland Typesetters, Australia

Printed and bound in Australia by Griffin Press, an accredited ISO AS/NZS 14001 Environmental Management Systems printer

A catalogue record for this book is available from the National Library of Australia

ISBN 978 1 76135 805 0

penguin.com.au

We at Penguin Random House Australia acknowledge that Aboriginal and Torres Strait Islander peoples are the first storytellers and Traditional Custodians of the land on which we live and work. We honour Aboriginal and Torres Strait Islander peoples' continuous connection to Country, waters, skies and communities. We celebrate Aboriginal and Torres Strait Islander stories, traditions and living cultures; and we pay our respects to Elders past and present.

CONTENTS

Introduction

> 'I've said many times before: we're at an inflection point. The post-Cold War period is over. A new era has begun.'
>
> President Joseph R. Biden, foreign policy remarks, State Department, 13 January 2025[1]

The United States' 2022 National Security Strategy declared that 'the post-Cold War era is definitively over and a competition is underway between the major powers to shape what comes next.'[2] In America, this sentiment is widely shared among Democrats and Republicans. But there is intense ideological competition in the United States to determine the type of order America should now try to create. This competition started after the Obama administration, which was the last restorationist

US government that sought to preserve the post-Cold War order largely as it was and without major changes to US strategy.

Donald Trump's first presidential term (2017–2021) seemed to be something of an aberration. He was a nationalist and a protectionist, but he was hemmed in by his cabinet officials, who tended to be more traditional conservative internationalists committed to alliances and a relatively open global economy. Trump took the United States in a very different direction, but by the end of his term, much of it seemed reversible and there was every possibility that the Republican standard-bearer in 2024 would be a conservative internationalist.

In office, Joe Biden spoke like a restorationist ('America is back') but did not govern as one. He broke with presidents Obama and Clinton in significant ways – on the Washington consensus for international economics, and on China and Russia. One can find in his administration a distinctive worldview for an era defined simultaneously by strategic competition with revisionist autocracies like Russia and China, and by interdependence.

When Trump came back, he changed course – embracing tariffs and economic warfare, sidelining great power competition, and flirting with territorial expansion. A new generation of America Firsters led by Vice President JD Vance began to lay out a worldview that is likely to endure in the Republican Party after Trump departs as president. This worldview does not always align with what Trump says and does.

This Paper seeks to discern those two worldviews – the emerging Democratic and America First perspectives – and their implications for world order, drawing on foreign policy in the Biden administration, in which I served as senior director for strategic planning at the National Security Council, and the first 12 months of the second Trump administration. Each administration acted decisively in very distinct ways.

During the Cold War, the United States pursued strategies of containment. As the historian John Lewis Gaddis has shown, there was some variance between these strategies from president to president and from party to party.[3] But what the strategies had in common – support for alliances, hostility to the Soviet Union, opposition to protectionism – was more important and significant. That is no longer the case. There is a vast difference between the emerging Democratic and America First worldviews.

The focus of this Paper is on what we have learned from the implementation of these two worldviews and what it reveals about how Democrats and

Republicans are likely to see the world in years to come.

Chapter 1 looks at what we learned about world order and Democratic foreign policy from the Russia–Ukraine war, while Chapter 2 asks the same questions for China strategy. Chapter 3 looks at Trump's trade and China policies, and Chapter 4 focuses on how Trump is handling alliances and partnerships. Finally, Chapter 5 considers the impact of these two worldviews on global order and how other countries are likely to react. The Trump chapters address events up until mid-February 2026, including the dramatic Delta Force raid to capture Venezuelan leader Nicolás Maduro and the transatlantic standoff over Greenland.

In many ways, Trump's return to the presidency confirmed the end not just of the post-Cold War order but of the order that was built and sustained by the United States after the Second World War based around alliances, economic integration, and strategic restraint. While remnants and champions of that order still exist, it has been shattered by the collapse of the American consensus and the rise of revisionist autocracies. We are now in a new world with two different Americas. Neither is likely to vanquish the other politically to chart a consistent course for decades. Instead, the country is likely to move back and forth between them.

If one looks back at American political history since 1944, Democrats have held the presidency for 40 years and Republicans are in their forty-second year. Essentially, the two parties have split the White House 50:50. There is no reason to expect that to change. But now, the geopolitical fluctuation that will occur when power changes hands is likely to be seismic.

The mere probability that such change will occur each time the presidency moves from one party to the other will itself have an impact on world politics. Can allies trust extended nuclear deterrence (America's promise to use nuclear weapons, if necessary, to defend an ally) if it is only likely to be provided half the time? How will countries structure their economies if 20 per cent tariffs are imposed and taken off every four or eight years? This ideological contest inside America, and the world's adjustment to it, will shape the international order for some time to come.

CHAPTER ONE

Indirect great power war

I joined the National Security Council (NSC) as senior director for strategic planning in April 2022, a couple of months after Russia invaded Ukraine. But from November 2021, I started to come in to see the National Security Adviser Jake Sullivan for conversations every few weeks. I had been in the White House only once before, for a West Wing tour several years prior. So when I went to see Sullivan the first time, it was a little surreal. I didn't know what exactly he wanted to talk about, so I made sure I was prepped with all of the administration's recent actions and public remarks.

Sullivan began by saying that he thought Russia would invade Ukraine but that the administration was doing everything possible to deter Moscow. He had set up a 'Tiger Team' to prepare plans to deal with an invasion. The administration was ready to send weapons to Ukraine and assist it in an insurgency against Russia if the invasion succeeded (which, at the time, many analysts believed was possible). It was also willing to engage in a serious diplomatic effort with the Russians to avert war, though only if that included Russian steps to reduce tensions. Sullivan was fairly sure those efforts would fail. 'What are we doing wrong, and what else could we do?' he asked me.

It was a revealing question. In Washington, when you're meeting a senior official, even one you know well and maybe especially then, it is customary to tell them they're doing a great job. I saw this all the time in government. But Sullivan had little interest in reflexive praise from close associates. He wanted constructive criticism, ideas, and plays. When they came up with something different, he would do his best to tear it apart. If their argument stood up to his scrutiny, he would embrace it. It was exhilarating and made our policy better, although some officials weren't too keen to go toe-to-toe with the national security adviser and second-guess the normal bureaucratic process.

We spoke about a few ideas. One was to frame the pending invasion as a flagrant violation of the UN Charter to rally the world to Ukraine's side. Another was to tell Russian president Vladimir Putin that if he invaded, the United States would support Swedish and Finnish membership of the North Atlantic Treaty Organization (NATO), which would greatly complicate Russia's security environment. But as Sullivan predicted, none of it deterred Russia. Putin was determined to have his war. 'Putin. What an asshole,' Sullivan remarked to me as he contemplated Europe's largest conflict since the Second World War.

A COLD WAR SIMMERING TO A BOIL

The Russia–Ukraine war was the dominating issue for me while I was at the NSC, taking up about 60 per cent of my time. I had a team of six, three of whom worked full-time on the war. And that was just in strategic planning. There were about 25 people on the NSC staff dealing with it (out of approximately 200), including our Russia and Europe teams, defence, intelligence, energy, press, arms control, and legislative affairs. We met with Sullivan every day to go over developments and plan the way forward.

I had believed for some time that the United States was in a long-term strategic competition with Russia and China, but the war took it to a whole new level. There had been nothing like it before, even during the Cold War. Yes, the Soviet Union and the United

States were involved in proxy wars where each backed the other's enemies, but this was a war right in the heart of Europe, on Russia's border. It wasn't a proxy war – Russia was the invader and Ukraine was choosing to fight back. Soviet casualties in Afghanistan were approximately 15,000 dead and 50,000 wounded from 1979 to 1987.[4] In Ukraine, they exceeded one million killed and injured by 2025, and were going up by about 1,500 every day.[5]

If Russia were to win, it would be well positioned to threaten Poland and the Baltic states. Putin was clear in the run-up to the war that he sought the withdrawal of foreign troops from all NATO countries added since 1997.[6] He would likely try to use the conquest of Ukraine to start a coercive diplomatic effort to weaken NATO. A Russian victory would also send a clear message to China and others that aggression could pay and the West would not act.

Biden was clear in his guidance.[7] He wanted to help Ukraine defeat Russian forces; he wanted to keep the NATO alliance united; and he wanted to avoid direct conflict with Russia. These three objectives were occasionally in tension. For example, if we established a no-fly zone, it would help Ukraine but it would also require US forces to shoot down Russian planes and strike Russian missile sites.

We settled on a policy of providing Ukraine with massive amounts of military assistance – some from our own stockpiles and some newly produced – and intelligence. We rallied our allies and partners, especially in Europe, to help. And we imposed crushing sanctions, including barring Russia from the SWIFT system, the global financial infrastructure that allows banks to send and receive payments. This policy remained in place for the duration of Biden's term.

One could write a whole book on the Biden administration's Ukraine policy, and I am sure some will. I would like to focus here on five things US support for Ukraine in the war told us about the future world order: the first is about the risk of nuclear use, the second is on escalation, the third is on the global nature of the war, the fourth is on the role of the Global South, and the fifth is on how to bring the war to an end.

THREE DAYS IN OCTOBER

In the first year of the war, Ukraine defied expectations by pushing Russian forces back from Kyiv, liberating more than half the territory it had initially lost in the invasion. In mid-to-late 2022, we received disturbing intelligence showing, as the journalist Bob Woodward later recounted in his book *War*, that 'Russian president Vladimir Putin was seriously considering using a tactical nuclear weapon' out of a sense of 'desperation over Russia's recent battlefield failures'.[8] It was unclear what precise circumstance would lead to nuclear use. Maybe it would be the destruction of the Russian army in Ukraine, but maybe it would be if Ukrainian forces took Crimea or were merely poised to take it.

As we formulated our response, one challenge was that the circumstances under which Russia might use nuclear weapons were precisely the circumstances we were trying to bring about: the defeat of Russian forces in Ukraine. We believed that pulling back from supporting Ukraine in response to this intelligence would not be in our interests, so we quickly decided to deter Putin by convincing him that resorting to nuclear use would leave Russia much worse off than before.

I helped coordinate our efforts, and over the northern summer, often on Saturdays, we convened regular and sometimes tense meetings and exercises in the White House Situation Room to game out the worst-case scenario and our likely response. In private channels with Russian officials, we said that nuclear use would result in catastrophic consequences for Russia.

The likelihood of nuclear-weapons use grew significantly in September and October of 2022. As

Woodward reported, the intelligence community assessed that if Russian forces were facing collapse in Ukraine, the probability of nuclear use was a coin flip.[9] So, we began to make our warnings public and we quietly spoke with China, India, and others.

The tensions culminated on the weekend of 21–23 October 2022. On Friday 21, Russian defence minister Sergei Shoigu finally agreed to take a call from defence secretary Lloyd Austin. It was only the second time they had spoken since the war started eight months before. According to Woodward's account of the call, Austin told Shoigu that any Russian use of nuclear weapons would be 'a world-changing event' that would implicate the national interests of the United States. It 'could set in motion events you cannot control and we cannot control . . . This could put us on the path of a confrontation'.[10]

Shoigu said Russia had no plans to use nuclear weapons, and that it was not consistent with their military doctrine. As we discussed with Jake Sullivan immediately after the call, the Russians lied to us constantly, but if they were going to use nuclear weapons soon, they would have used the call to lay a pretext. So, Shoigu's denial was possibly a sign that nuclear use was not imminent.

But any hope that the call with Shoigu bought us some time was shattered 24 hours later on

Saturday evening. We got a message from our Pentagon colleagues to say that Shoigu had requested an urgent call with Austin for Sunday morning. No calls in four months and now two in 48 hours? Something was up.

When we woke early Sunday morning, the United Kingdom, France, and Turkey had received similar messages. The Russian media was awash with stories about Ukraine preparing to use a dirty bomb against Russia. This could be the pretext for nuclear use that we feared. Emergency meetings followed that Sunday. As David Ignatius of *The Washington Post* reported, Biden sent a letter to Putin warning against nuclear use and proposing a meeting between the director of the CIA, William Burns, and whomever Vladimir Putin chose.[11] We worked with the Ukrainians to invite the International Atomic Energy Agency (IAEA) into Ukraine to verify that there was no dirty bomb.

It was a rocky 24 hours but Putin accepted the offer of a meeting. The IAEA debunked the Russian accusations. China and India came out publicly against nuclear use in the conflict. Ukraine gained some territory, but unfortunately, Russian forces did not collapse. The risk of nuclear use receded.

The lesson I took from this episode is that throughout the nuclear era there had been little conceptual or policy work done on preventing a nuclear power from using nuclear weapons against a country that wasn't formally allied with the United States and therefore wasn't covered by Washington's nuclear 'umbrella'. Such an event would not just be catastrophic for the country attacked; if the attack achieved its objectives, it could also normalise the use of nuclear weapons in limited wars and lead to a new round of proliferation. I believe we handled this threat reasonably well, although we can never know for sure why the Russians chose not to use nuclear weapons. Nevertheless, this episode highlighted a danger that could easily re-emerge in the future, and it underscored the necessity of an active US role if we want to avert nuclear use for the first time since the Second World War.

ESCALATION MANAGEMENT

One of the persistent critiques of our policy was that we were deterred by an empty Russian threat of escalation and failed to send Ukraine what it needed to win – namely, more weapons, faster, and without any restrictions on their use. This aggravated us because we felt we were moving heaven and earth every day to get Ukraine everything we could. More importantly though, and setting our feelings aside, it was not an accurate reflection of our thinking about the risks of Russia using nuclear weapons or Russian escalation more generally, and it obscures the real lessons from the war for conflicts of the future.

We created an entire apparatus to help Ukraine fight, including supplying arms from our stockpiles, procuring new arms and equipment, setting up the logistical system to get it to Ukraine in a timely manner, and providing intelligence and military cooperation.[12] This was unprecedented, and it was all set up in the first couple of months of the war. There were logistical and bureaucratic hurdles that sometimes resulted in small delays, but by any reasonable metric the policy was rapidly turned into reality.

The funds we had at our disposal from Congress to help Ukraine defend itself were large, but they were also finite. Each month, we had to decide how best to spend them, which required us to assess what the Ukrainians needed most at any particular moment. The two priorities throughout most of the war were artillery, which was critically important for the front lines, and air defences to shoot down Russian aircraft, drones, and missiles.

The air defences included Patriot systems but, given the scale of the Russian attacks, that was not enough. It made no sense to use an expensive Patriot missile to shoot down a cheap drone. Ukraine needed layered air defences that included other types of missiles as well as electronic warfare systems to jam Russian radar and communications, and counter-drone systems.

The artillery ammunition Ukraine needed was mainly 155 mm rounds, of which we did not have many. At the start of the conflict, we were producing 14,000 a month but Ukraine was using between 4,000 and 6,000 a day.[13] We upped production but the supply of critical components, particularly the precursor material used for the explosive, was scarce. As a result, we scoured the world to find partners willing to send rounds to Ukraine, sometimes indirectly by selling them to us first.

This prioritisation meant that we sometimes rejected flashier expensive items that Kyiv pressed for but which our military assessed would not be particularly helpful on the battlefield. A good example was the F-16 fighter plane, which Kyiv was desperate to acquire. Europe had a decent supply of these. They are expensive, so we believed it made sense to have the Netherlands, Denmark, Belgium, and Norway provide them to Ukraine, and we would preserve the funds we had for other items that only the United States could supply, such as mid- and long-range rockets and missiles, air defences, and artillery. The other problem was that F-16s require highly trained pilots fluent in English.

Ukraine had fewer than 20 eligible for training, which would itself take more than a year.[14] Pilot availability was a far greater constraint than the aircraft themselves. For that reason, the F-16s Ukraine acquired took some time to enter the war, and often did so in a limited way.

The most controversial weapon was the Army Tactical Missile System, known as ATACMS, that has a 300 km range (there are also shorter-range variants). Ukraine wanted to use it to strike inside Russia. Out of every weapon we supplied, this was the only one the Russians explicitly warned us about, saying that allowing its use against targets in Russia would result in significant escalation. Since we did not have a massive supply of ATACMS, we judged that we could be taking on significant escalation risk for little tangible gain. Here, it is fair to say that the escalation concern was a factor in our decision-making.

We had already provided a shorter-range variant of ATACMS for use against Russian forces in Crimea. These missiles had disrupted Russian supply lines but they did not move the front lines, which remained fairly static thanks to land mines, the use of so-called tree line defences (whereby a line of trees is used for camouflage and protection), and increasingly the use of drones to watch and hit infantry.

The Ukrainians would complain that escalation fears were unfounded because the Russians were doing everything they could inside Ukraine anyway. Ukraine was understandably focused on 'vertical' escalation, whereby Russia would up the ante in Ukraine, but we could see numerous vectors for 'horizontal' escalation, whereby Russia would target American interests elsewhere – as reported by the media, Russia was looking at providing the Houthis with advanced missiles to strike our ships in the Red Sea, and Russian agents were suspected of plotting to place flammable devices on planes.[15]

We also believed that not providing ATACMS gave us room to escalate in other ways without triggering a Russian escalation in kind. In other words, keeping this one capability in reserve gave the perception of restraint regardless of what else we did. It was letting us boil the proverbial frog. When we did introduce a new weapon system or escalate in some other way, we would sometimes give Moscow an ultimatum to reverse some new escalation of their own, making it clear that they bore responsibility for the intensification of the conflict.

We did ultimately authorise the use of ATACMS against targets inside Russia in response to North Korea's intervention in the war. We had warned the Russians against taking this step and told them there would be a commensurate response. ATACMS helped Ukraine strike North Korean forces as they were gathering to fight, as well as hitting their command posts.

Escalation management was not a constraint that prevented action but a framework that enabled us to significantly increase our support for Ukraine while limiting Russia's response as much as possible. Many analysts conflated escalation management with other dynamics, including which weapons to prioritise, how to maintain readiness in other theatres, and concerns about inadvertent technology transfer to Russia and China. The bottom line, though, is that the scale and scope of our assistance would have been unthinkable at the start of the war.

THE END OF ARMS CONTROL

In June 2023, as Ukraine's counteroffensive was beginning to stall, the Ukrainians were running out of artillery, and this time there was no external supply that could fill the gap. We had seen this coming for months and there was a solution: we could give the Ukrainians cluster munitions, weapons that disperse multiple smaller explosive submunitions, or 'bomblets', over a wide area. Cluster munitions have been banned by much of the world, including by our European allies, in the Convention on Cluster Munitions concluded in Dublin in 2008 because unexploded bomblets can accumulate on the battlefield and kill civilians long after a war comes to an end. The United States had not joined the Convention largely because of the demands of war plans on the Korean Peninsula. The United States was no longer producing cluster munitions, but there was a large stockpile.

It was an incredibly tough issue and a wrenching decision. Everyone knew the human cost these munitions could inflict over time. We would take heat for shredding what many considered to be an important arms control treaty. However, the military believed cluster munitions would be effective against the invading force and, since Ukraine was running out of other munitions, the choice was to either give Ukraine cluster weapons or accept a massive Russian advantage in firepower. In the end, the NSC staff were of the view that since the cluster munitions would be used inside Ukraine it was really the prerogative of the democratically elected Ukrainian government to weigh the long-term risk to civilians (in areas already saturated with explosives, including Russian cluster munitions) against the near-term risk of a brutal Russian advance and occupation further into Ukraine.

President Biden agreed with this logic and the necessity of providing cluster munitions given the lack of an alternative. It would give us time to ramp up the defence industrial base so it could produce enough regular munitions each month. We still took a lot of heat. I was one of two briefers on a call with arms control experts who were appalled, but not a single one offered an alternative. They insisted that we should have found some better path forward, though what that path might have been eluded them.

We had a similar issue with landmines, which had been banned by the Ottawa Convention following a campaign spearheaded by Princess Diana. During the Ukrainian counteroffensive, the Russians deployed vast quantities of landmines. They were brutally effective in stopping the Ukrainian advance. In 2024, as the Ukrainians were running out of frontline troops, significant areas were thinly defended. There was little doubt that landmines would be effective, so again we faced a gut-wrenching decision. We had produced non-persistent landmines that become inert after a certain period of time. President Biden hesitated but ultimately decided to transfer them to Ukraine because they were undoubtedly necessary to its defence.

By mid-2025, many countries in Eastern Europe had withdrawn from both the cluster munition and landmine conventions because they knew they might also need these weapons if the Russians invaded. These conventions were the product of a particular geopolitical moment, one of relative peace and great power cooperation. They made the world a better place. But when the geopolitical environment deteriorated, the treaties fell apart.

Meanwhile, the Russians had not only made full use of cluster munitions and landmines from the beginning of the war, they were also undermining the nuclear arms control regime carefully built up over decades. Moscow effectively suspended the 2010 New START Treaty to limit the Russian and American nuclear arsenals. It revised its nuclear doctrine to say Russia could use nuclear weapons against a nuclear state that was assisting its adversary in a war (in the way the United States, the United Kingdom, and France were helping Ukraine).[16] It developed and used a missile called Oreshnik, the first ever wartime use of a weapon that can deploy multiple, independently targetable nuclear and conventional warheads.[17] And, US officials believed Russia was developing plans to deploy a nuclear weapon in space to hold satellites at risk.[18]

All of this reminded us daily that we were in a dangerous new era with rival powers, and that the old days where we could negotiate imperfect limits on arms on both sides were likely a thing of the past.

THE GLOBAL DIMENSIONS OF THE CONFLICT – WEST VERSUS EAST

Like the Spanish Civil War in the 1930s, the Russia–Ukraine war has had global significance. Countries were pulled into supporting their preferred side, seeing larger issues at stake.

Ukraine was a beneficiary of the globalisation of the war. The United States and Europe led the way by providing Ukraine with vast quantities of weapons, intelligence support, and economic assistance, but democracies in the Indo-Pacific also played a significant role. South Korea indirectly sent Ukraine approximately half a million rounds of ammunition, Japan gave Ukraine more than US$12 billion in financial assistance and non-lethal defence equipment (such as heavy vehicles and anti-drone technology), and Australia gave lethal assistance including tanks, armoured vehicles, and loitering munitions. Elsewhere, Israel gave permission for US ammunition stored there to be transferred to Ukraine (prior to 7 October 2023). There were also countless deals with countries that provided assistance but wanted to remain anonymous.[19]

Russia also put together a formidable coalition, with China in the lead. In the run-up to the war, Putin and Chinese president Xi Jinping met and signed a so-called 'no-limits partnership'. It is unlikely that Putin laid out his full plan to Xi, but the Chinese leader knew he was going to do something. Once the war started, China's overarching interest was to ensure that Russia did not fail. China needed Russia as a partner in its struggle against the United States. Xi could only be guaranteed this if Putin was running Russia. If Putin fell, who knows what a future Russian leader might do. The most likely pathway to a change in regime was defeat in the war, so China needed to prevent that from happening. China looked at providing lethal assistance but backed off under pressure from the West. China ended up helping Russia reconstitute its military and defence industrial base much more rapidly than would otherwise have been the case. This included the provision of machine tools, microelectronics, and other technology as well as undertaking co-production of drones with Russia.[20]

North Korea initially rejected Putin's request for help but later agreed. Pyongyang then sent millions of artillery rounds as well as ballistic missiles, multiple-launch rocket systems, and long-range artillery.[21] It also sent approximately 12,000 troops to fight in the Kursk region in 2024.[22] Iran sent Shahed drones and advisers to get the Russians accustomed to using them, and then helped Russia set up its own drone production lines.

Why were China, Iran, and North Korea helping Russia? Part of the answer, we believed, lay in what Moscow was sending in the other direction. Russia was providing invaluable technological and military assistance to all three countries. It was giving more to get more in return – call it strategic transactionalism. In essence, we were seeing a deep military integration between Russia and each of these countries. It wasn't necessarily a commitment to coordinate aggression, but it went far further than anyone expected.

A FRACTURED GLOBAL SOUTH

The world was not just split in two over Ukraine. There were many countries in the so-called Global South (a term everyone hated but to which no one could find a catchy alternative) that tried to portray themselves as opposed to Russia's invasion and to the Western alliance backing Ukraine. Their rationale was that support for Ukraine's membership of NATO was a contributing factor to the conflict, never mind that when Russia invaded in 2022, there was no prospect of Ukraine joining NATO anytime soon. In 2023, a number of countries started to discuss the need to bring the war to an end. Brazil, China, and South Africa all produced plans or began talking about negotiations to end the war. We did not have any hope for these efforts, but we saw some risk in simply opposing or criticising them as pointless. So, we opted for a different tack.

We were positive about all efforts to end the war but we would also remind those leaders that it would be an extremely difficult process and they needed to put in the work if they wanted to make a difference. If a leader from the Global South wanted to meet with Putin, we would encourage them to also meet with Ukrainian president Volodymyr Zelenskyy. We would say that any deal must be compatible with the UN Charter, of which they were all publicly supportive. We felt this was right on the merits but also avoided a situation where the West was portrayed as the 'continue the war' party while a Russian-leaning group of Global South countries was in favour of ending it.

The main actors in the Global South responded in different ways to our challenge. China had little interest in trying to bring the war to an end, but it wanted to be perceived as doing exactly that. Beijing came up with a 12-point plan. It was not a serious document in that it did not grapple with any of the real sticking points: territory, Ukraine's need for security guarantees, and reparations. That said, it had some positive elements, and we did not want to be seen as rejecting it. So, we welcomed China's initiative and said there were some points we agreed with while others gave us concern. Point 1 in the plan stated:

> **Respecting the sovereignty of all countries.** Universally recognized international law, including the purposes and principles of the United Nations Charter, must be strictly observed. The sovereignty, independence and territorial integrity of all countries must be effectively upheld. All countries, big or small, strong or weak, rich or poor, are equal members of the international community. All parties should jointly uphold the basic norms governing international relations and defend international fairness and justice. Equal and uniform application of international law should be promoted, while double standards must be rejected.[23]

It was clear to us that Beijing had included this out of fear that if the norm of territorial revisionism was established, it could weaken their claim to Taiwan. The rest of the document tilted more towards Russia with headings that included 'Abandoning the Cold War mentality' and 'Stopping unilateral sanctions'. So, whenever we talked about China's plan, we were always careful to say that there were some points we agreed with, such as point 1, and use that to underscore Russia's violations of the UN Charter. This made Beijing uncomfortable, but they had no easy way out. China never had any intention of putting pressure on Russia to compromise or to engage in meaningful talks. It was all for show.

The Brazilians, particularly President Luiz Inácio Lula da Silva and his national security adviser Celso Amorim, were ideologically aligned with the Russians. Lula hadn't thought much about what a settlement would look like or how it could endure, but he liked the idea of being perceived as statesman and peacemaker. He was always careful not to deviate from the Russian position, and sometimes this backfired. In April 2023, he visited Washington and met with President Biden. We told him that the United States did not expect Brazil to take sides against China or Russia, but we hoped that it would also not take sides against us. We encouraged Brazil to work for peace in Ukraine, but we wanted Lula to engage with Zelenskyy as well as Putin.

Shortly thereafter, Lula went to China to meet Xi Jinping. While in Beijing he said, 'The United

States needs to stop encouraging war and start talking about peace.' In Shanghai, he criticised the dollar, saying, 'Every night I ask myself why all countries have to base their trade on the dollar?'[24] Jake Sullivan was furious, telling me it was disrespectful after Biden had been such a gracious host to Lula. Things soon got worse. When Lula returned home, Brazil hosted Russian foreign minister Sergey Lavrov. In a joint media conference, Brazil's foreign minister Mauro Vieira criticised Western sanctions on Russia while Lavrov spoke about a shared Russian–Brazilian perspective on the war. This sparked a backlash in Brazil. *O Globo*, one of its largest circulation newspapers, ran an editorial titled 'Lula's "neutrality" reveals tacit support for Russia'.[25] *O Globo* was generally critical of Lula but other outlets more favourable to him faulted his stance on the war too. Lula's government found itself on the defensive, arguing that there had been no breach with the United States – we made it clear in background briefings that there had been. After that overreach, Lula and Amorim were a bit more circumspect.

At one point, a South African delegation came to see Sullivan and admonished the administration for not being more interested in a peace settlement. Sullivan pointed out that rewarding Russia with territorial gains over the heads of the Ukrainians would set a dangerous precedent, including for South Africa. The delegation agreed completely – there could be no compromise over territorial integrity. What they had in mind was a five-year freeze on Ukrainian membership of NATO in exchange for a full Russian withdrawal from Ukrainian territory. Needless to say, we would have taken that deal without hesitation.

The South Africans then organised a delegation of African leaders to visit Russia. We encouraged them to also go to Kyiv but we were concerned that the Ukrainians might give them the cold shoulder while the Russians would roll out the red carpet. We needn't have worried. The African delegation went to both capitals. The Russians helpfully bombed Kyiv when the African leaders were in the Ukrainian capital, while the Ukrainians engaged them constructively. On their trip to Moscow, by contrast, the Russians made it clear they did not really want external help in ending the conflict, and South African president Cyril Ramaphosa spoke publicly about Ukraine's territorial integrity. We felt that our constructive engagement with the Global South was bearing fruit.

OUR DIPLOMATIC CHALLENGE

Pointing out the shortcomings of the Global South's peace plans was one thing, but we still needed a plan of our own to end the war. It was clear to us that it had to end through negotiations. Even if Ukraine regained all of its territory, including Crimea, Russia could choose to continue fighting from its own territory. The war is not a race with a finish line that ends once Ukraine reaches its internationally recognised borders. We believed we had to put Ukraine in the strongest possible position on the battlefield for a future negotiation.

After the failed counteroffensive of 2023, we were dubious that Ukraine would be able to retake large swathes of territory from the Russians. The persistent use of drones made it very difficult to manoeuvre. The Ukrainians had not been able to execute large-scale combined arms operations and they were short on manpower. Therefore, we favoured a primarily defensive strategy that demonstrated to Russia that it could not make any more gains and would pay a massive price for continuing to fight, while Ukraine would continue to take opportunities for smaller tactical gains that would accumulate over time.

The Ukrainians tended more towards the 'knock-out blow' theory of victory. They would do something spectacular to demonstrate to the Russians and their allies, especially China, the futility of the invasion. Throughout 2024, Andriy Yermak, then head of Ukraine's presidential office and often considered the second-most powerful person in its government, kept telling us that they planned to hold a major peace summit in late 2024 at which Ukraine would present a plan to Russia that the rest of the world would back and that Moscow would have no choice but to accept. We were sceptical that Russia's partners would ever put any pressure on Moscow to end the war or that Putin would listen to them anyway.

To us, the primary problem to be solved in negotiations was that Russia wanted a neutered and weakened Ukraine whereas Ukraine wanted sufficient security capabilities and guarantees to deter and defend against any future attack. Putin laid out Russia's demands plainly in a July 2021 essay denying that Ukraine was a real country, in a speech to the Russian Ministry of Foreign Affairs in June 2024, and, after Biden left office, in Russia's formal proposal for negotiations in Istanbul in June 2025. The substance was always the same: territorial concessions, demilitarisation, no Western support for Ukraine and, effectively, regime change in Kyiv.[26]

Therefore, the challenge for the United States and its allies was to work with Kyiv to agree on a settlement that provided for a free and independent Ukraine with the ability to defend itself and deter a future attack, and then to persuade Putin to accept it. We were of the view that for negotiations to succeed, we would have to create a reality on the ground that convinced Putin he could not win and that continuing to fight would weaken Russia globally. We hoped that if Kamala Harris won the 2024 presidential election and made clear that US support to Ukraine would continue, it could create an opening for negotiations in 2025.

I helped coordinate our work on post-war planning. We looked at several different end-states. Our two preferred options were what we called the Norway model and the Israel model. In the Norway model, Ukraine could join NATO but it would agree to limits on foreign bases, troops, naval vessels, and equipment in the country. Given that Russia would be making such a significant concession, there could be a negotiation with the Russians on limits to Ukraine's military and new discussions on security architecture, such as the positioning of forces.

In the Israel model, the United States would provide Ukraine with enough military and intelligence assistance to enable it to defeat Russian forces without direct intervention by other nations. This would include effective air defences, an air force with a significant number of F-16s, stockpiles of munitions, a trained force capable of combined arms operations, robust defences along a negotiated line of control, long-range missiles, and a resilient and cutting-edge defence industrial base to produce as much as possible in country.

We believed that we should aim for Norway but settle for Israel. We thought the Norway model would present Russia with a real dilemma because while Moscow was opposed to NATO membership, a Ukraine with an external security guarantee would likely be more restrained than one that was on its own.

Ultimately, we were unable to get negotiations up and running before the end of Biden's term. We believed at the time that Putin had little interest in talking. He was willing to pay an enormous cost to win, and he thought he would get a better deal under Trump. As events unfolded in 2025, we felt vindicated on that score.

A QUESTION OF AMERICAN POWER

The Russia–Ukraine war is something of a Rorschach test. To some, it demonstrates the limits of American power. By the end of the Biden administration and after almost three years of support, Ukraine had failed to expel Russian forces from its territory and the war raged on. However, many of us who served in the Biden administration drew the opposite conclusion. The war was a testament to American power.

With no US troops involved and a cost of less than 4 per cent of overall US defence spending for that period, the United States helped Ukraine stave off a much larger power armed with nuclear weapons. By 2025, Russia was bogged down in eastern Ukraine, grinding out small territorial gains but haemorrhaging approximately 1,500 casualties a day, with no clear pathway forward if the West stood alongside Ukraine.

The United States has learned many lessons from the war – on the nature of modern land warfare, on the role of drones and artificial intelligence, on deterrence and escalation management, on war termination, and on managing a partner directly involved in a conflict. Not all of those lessons can be directly applied to other theatres and scenarios, but the experience is likely to shape all those who have been involved in it – political appointees, career civil servants, and the military.

CHAPTER TWO

Managed competition

A BALLOON FROM THE BLUE

I was in Jake Sullivan's office on the night of Tuesday 30 January 2023 for his evening wrap meeting, a daily round-up of what happened over the course of the day and what might lie ahead. The wrap conversation was typically informal and frank, and often went in unexpected directions.

One of the updates was about a Chinese spy balloon that had been spotted off the coast of Alaska over the weekend and ended up in Canada. It had now crossed back into the United States, was over Montana, and was on course to fly across the country. It appeared to be gathering intelligence as it went. Sullivan was alarmed and went around the room to see who was in favour of shooting it down immediately. Most of us were, as was he. Other departments and agencies had concerns, though. The intelligence community felt that it stood to learn more by observing the balloon, especially if Beijing did not know we could see it. The military was worried its altitude of approximately 18,000 metres was such that, if it fell, it could land anywhere in a 50 square kilometre area, potentially killing innocents on the ground.

President Biden gave the order on Wednesday to shoot the balloon down. At the last minute, the chairman of the joint chiefs of staff, General Mark Milley, warned him that it could result in civilian casualties, so it was agreed to wait until it had passed the East Coast and was over water. We had already locked down all sensitive sites so China would not gain any intelligence. We informed Congress, which meant it was just a matter of time before the news became public, although some eagle-eyed plane watchers were already asking questions online about flight restrictions at Billings airport in Montana, which had been imposed to facilitate an Air Force operation to take the balloon out. We began to plan our response. The Pentagon told us that on its current course and speed, the balloon would be over Washington, DC, on Tuesday, which happened to be the day of the State of the Union address. I conjured images of a

TV split screen, the president making his way to the Capitol in one half and the spy balloon in the other.

Secretary of State Antony Blinken was supposed to be travelling to China that weekend. Initially, he was keen to keep the engagement – to read them the riot act and show that diplomatic channels remained open. But the spy balloon was not yet public. Many of us believed that once that happened, all hell would break loose domestically while Blinken was en route. He decided to postpone.

On Thursday, we waited for the story to break. I searched Twitter for the word 'balloon'. There were a handful of references. I knew that within an hour or two, it would be all anyone could talk about. A media frenzy ensued. The balloon reached the ocean on Saturday afternoon, 4 February. At 2.39 p.m. Eastern Time, with the world watching, an F-22 Raptor shot it down with a Sidewinder missile.[27]

The balloon incident took place after a turbulent few months. In August 2022, over our objections, House Speaker Nancy Pelosi had visited Taiwan, giving China a pretext for a massive escalation in its military operations around the island, including firing missiles over it. In October 2022, we had announced the first technological export controls on advanced semiconductor chips to China. And we were closely tracking the possibility that China would supply Russia with lethal assistance in its war against Ukraine. We knew we were in an intense strategic competition with China, but the Pelosi visit and the balloon were a reminder of the enormous impact of unexpected events and of how quickly things could turn bad. It was not where we expected to be.

THE ORIGINS OF MANAGED COMPETITION

In his first term, President Trump's National Security Strategy declared that great power competition was America's primary national security challenge. However, his administration was divided between hawks who wanted to act against China on that premise and dealmakers who wanted to strike an economic bargain with Beijing. It was also constrained by Trump's visceral suspicion of alliances and his opposition to a wider order-shaping mission for the United States. In the final year of his first term, as the US–China relationship deteriorated partly as a result of Covid, the hawks gained the upper hand and took some competitive actions against Beijing, but the overall strategy remained a mixed bag.

When Biden took office, he had a choice. He could build on what Trump had left on China – mainly a legacy of prioritising competition over engagement – or he could return to President Barack Obama's approach. Obama understood that the United States and China were geopolitical competitors and he had several prominent hawks on his team, but he did not want his policy to be completely defined by geopolitics. Obama sought to balance competition and cooperation and was confident that the United States could deal with China without major disruptions to US domestic or foreign policy.

During Trump's first term, many of those who served in the Obama administration wrote extensively about China policy, arguing that America should take strategic competition with China much more seriously. Kurt Campbell and Ely Ratner wrote that Washington 'put too much faith in its power to shape China's trajectory . . . All sides of the policy debate erred,' they said, including 'free traders and financiers who foresaw inevitable and increasing openness in China, integrationists who argued that Beijing's ambitions would be tamed by greater interaction with the international community, and hawks who believed that China's power would be abated by perpetual American primacy.'[28]

At this time, Rush Doshi – then a scholar at the Brookings Institution who would go on to serve in the Biden administration – was writing an influential book called *The Long Game*, in which he used primary source documents to show that Beijing had a plan to displace the United States as global leader.[29] Organisations such as the Center for Security and Emerging Technology at Georgetown University and the Center for a New American Security laid out a case for tighter export controls and investments in domestic capabilities to counter Beijing's growing technological capabilities. Many think tanks also argued for a revival and strengthening of US alliances.[30]

Some leading Democrats believed that unbridled competition with China ran the risk of precipitating a major crisis before the United States was properly prepared. It was better, they thought, to invest in national strength, build an alliance system that would make it more difficult for China to pursue an aggressive regional policy, and methodically and consistently implement a competitive strategy. To borrow the title from Kurt Campbell and Jake Sullivan's piece in *Foreign Affairs*, the Biden team wanted 'competition without catastrophe' – in other words, competitive actions that could be calibrated in a way that avoided a dangerous spiral into confrontation, crisis, and conflict.[31] This provided the basis for the strategy that would become known as managed competition.

The administration's China strategy, which drew on all these contributions, was completed by the time I joined the NSC. But some doctrinal questions did arise during the drafting of the National Security Strategy, for which I was responsible.[32]

The first was on prioritisation. Could we say China was our top priority even after Russia had invaded Ukraine? And how could we show that we were really committed to rebalancing US strategy to the Indo-Pacific? To us, the notion that America's alliances in Europe came at the expense of our alliances in the Indo-Pacific, or the Middle East for that matter, was a false paradigm. Our alliances are a strategic asset. Europe can and does help us in the Indo-Pacific. Our allies in Asia have helped us with Russia. It's important that we keep our allies in the Middle East on board for our competition with China. We often spoke, including in the National Security Strategy, about growing the connective tissue between our alliances in different regions. The National Security Strategy emphasised that China is 'the only competitor with both the intent to reshape the international order and, increasingly, the economic, diplomatic, military, and technological power to advance that objective.'[33] This, we hoped, would convey that we understood China was the largest challenge we faced.

The second question was on whether to frame the competition with China in terms of autocracy and democracy. Biden constantly spoke about a global struggle between the two. He often brought it up in ad hoc remarks, which was a telling sign that it meant a lot to him. This was probably the most divisive doctrinal issue among administration officials when I joined. Some on the Middle East and Asia teams worried that it would make it more difficult to work with non-democracies like Saudi Arabia and Vietnam. Others worried that it would make US–China competition too ideological and zero-sum. On the other hand, there was little doubt that China was becoming more authoritarian and increasingly comfortable with advancing an illiberal vision of world order in partnership with Russia.

I felt the document needed to reflect the president's worldview. It would be absurd to airbrush his talk of autocracy versus democracy from the record, especially since he had no intention of dropping it. Our job was to explain and unpack his policy, not to deny it. In the National Security Strategy, we embraced the concept but explained that 'the most pressing strategic challenge facing' the United States 'is from powers that layer authoritarian governance with a revisionist foreign policy'.[34] These states wage wars of aggression, undermine democracies, engage in economic coercion, and export an illiberal model of international order. We recognised that many non-democracies join the world's democracies in forswearing these behaviours, and we could partner with them, but Russia and China do not.

The final issue was on the tension between strategic competition and cooperation on shared challenges. Some people, especially external experts, worried that focusing on strategic competition would make cooperation impossible. We thought that was naive. China had little interest in cooperating with us on anything, at least not on terms we considered acceptable. Beijing wanted us to accommodate its so-called 'core interests', a term China uses to define non-negotiables such as the status of Tibet and Taiwan, if we were to work together on issues such as climate change.

In the National Security Strategy, we said that America faced two interrelated challenges: the first was strategic competition with China and the second was a set of shared challenges such as pandemics, climate change, and artificial intelligence. There is a negative synergy between the two, in that geopolitical competition can make it harder to cooperate on shared challenges, while shared challenges can exacerbate geopolitical rivalries. We could not just wish one away – for example, by prioritising cooperation with China over competition. We needed to tackle both. That meant we should always be clear that we stood willing to work with China without geopolitical preconditions but that we should not expect Beijing to reciprocate. We had to have a backup plan – to forge coalitions of the willing with like-minded nations to deal with our shared challenges.

THREE BIG BREAKS WITH THE PAST

If one surveys the term of the administration, there were three ways in which Biden broke from both Obama and Trump on China policy, putting the ideas described above into action. There wasn't unanimous agreement on these policies – parts of the bureaucracy were uneasy with aspects of each – but they are perceived by most of the Democratic foreign policy establishment to have been a success, and they are likely to remain part of its agenda in 2029 if Democrats come back to power.

The first departure is that Biden deepened alliances in ways that increased national and collective capabilities and went far beyond better atmospherics or more meetings. Agreements were signed to increase America's access to military bases in Australia, Japan, Papua New Guinea, and the Philippines. US cooperation with India reached a historic high, yielding agreements on defence production, technology, and civil nuclear regulations. The administration also sought to manage and minimise disagreements with New Delhi to build out the overall geopolitical relationship. The Biden administration elevated the Quad (a dialogue between the United States, Japan, India, and Australia) to the leaders' level and empowered it. It also created two separate trilateral forums – one with South Korea and Japan, and the other with the Philippines and Japan. It was a period of genuine transformation in the US alliance system in the region.

AUKUS – the agreement for the United States, Australia, and the United Kingdom to build nuclear-powered submarines for Australia, replacing Canberra's previous deal with France – was bold and audacious. It was more than just an arms sale. The new submarines will enable Australia to conduct operations in Northeast Asia, not just Southeast Asia. It will link America's Indo-Pacific and Atlantic alliances. It also contains a second pillar encouraging cooperation on advanced technologies. AUKUS symbolises the integration of the allied submarine industrial base that many Biden administration officials believed was where the alliance system needed to go. The idea was pitched by the Morrison government and came to fruition within the National Security Council, particularly via Indo-Pacific coordinator Kurt Campbell and Jake Sullivan. Given the sensitivity, it was kept a very close hold.

The NSC team briefed it to the president. Biden was supportive and saw it as strengthening an important alliance. However, he was also cautious. He wanted to make sure it did not damage the non-proliferation regime, which it did not. Yet he did not fully appreciate the scale of the controversy that would ensue. Once the deal was announced, all hell broke loose. The French government was apoplectic and withdrew its ambassadors from Washington and Canberra. Paris framed it as a crisis for the transatlantic relationship, which was, of course, a top priority for the president.

There is now a widely held view that it was a mistake not to bring France into the conversation earlier and buy them off with the promise of some involvement. But that was never going to fly. If France had caught a whiff of AUKUS, it would have mobilised all of its considerable resources to destroy it before it was announced. Paris would likely have found some support for their position within the administration from those who valued the transatlantic relationship over alliances in the Indo-Pacific. Had the president foreseen the intensity of French anger, it is also very possible that he would have chosen not to go ahead with the deal. Thankfully, with the agreement signed and sealed, there was no turning back.

France milked the AUKUS controversy for everything it was worth from a penitent administration, even getting a state dinner. The president said publicly that what happened was 'clumsy and not done with a lot of grace' and that he thought France had been informed in advance that their submarine deal with Australia was not moving forward.[35] The administration endorsed France's concept of European strategic autonomy as long as it was pursued in a way that was complementary to NATO, and launched a series of strategic dialogues with Paris. Campbell was in the doghouse for a little while. But excruciating as all this was, the important thing was that AUKUS moved forward.

China detested the deepening of alliances, especially AUKUS, the Enhanced Defence Cooperation Agreement with the Philippines, and the trilateral dialogue between the United States, Japan, and South Korea, which was designed to overcome the mutual suspicion and antagonism between our Northeast Asian allies. It created a real dilemma for Beijing – the tougher they acted towards the region, the tighter the alliances became. If they tried to respond by imposing additional costs, that merely reinforced the dynamic. We knew it and sought to take full advantage of Beijing's assertiveness to strengthen our alliance system.

The second departure from Obama and Trump's first term was on technological competition. Trump had imposed restrictions on Huawei's involvement in 5G networks, including putting it on the entity list, which effectively barred US companies from supplying it without a licence. The Trump administration put pressure on other countries to follow suit and tried to limit China's access to equipment that would allow it to rival the United States in chip building. But these were relatively modest steps and did not stop China from buying advanced chips from the United States.

The Biden team believed that the world was on the cusp of a revolution in artificial intelligence and that, if China were to win it, it could upend the balance of power by giving it military and technological advantages over the United States. China had enough talent and it also had a couple of distinct advantages – it had more access to data than US firms and it could provide state support to its companies. The one area where it was at a relative disadvantage to the United States was in computing power. The Biden administration would make this its focus. On 7 October 2022, the Biden administration introduced the first tranche of export controls, preventing US tech company Nvidia from selling its best chips to China. And in January 2023, late on a Friday night and with no formal announcement or fanfare, administration officials signed an agreement with Japan and the Netherlands, the two other leading nations on equipment for semiconductor manufacturing, to introduce parallel controls.[36]

Nvidia immediately started to work on a chip that went right up to the new line without crossing it, breaching the spirit if not the letter of the law. So, we updated the restrictions annually to make it clear that we would play whack-a-mole if needed. The controls created some anxiety in China and among allies in Asia and Europe that we were moving towards a broader economic decoupling. Some of this concern was genuine but some was used instrumentally to undermine the case for export controls. We went to great lengths to emphasise that the controls would be highly targeted and limited to the most advanced chips and investments that could be used to train frontier AI models. Jake Sullivan started using the term 'small yard, high fence' to describe our approach. Critics said the yard was continuously expanding, but we felt it was self-evident that the controls would have to adjust as China, Nvidia, and others sought workarounds. The benefit of the term was that it clearly signalled that the export controls would be used in special cases and not applied across the economic relationship.

Biden's third major shift away from his predecessors' policies was to detach himself from the neoliberal approaches to the global economy that had characterised the Clinton and Obama administrations. Much of the rationale for this change had to do with China. In the 1940s, the United States built an economic order of nations to help them recover from the Second World War and to prevent a return to the protectionism of the 1930s. This order also helped create an alliance system that could contain the Soviet Union. After the Cold War, this order expanded to include most of the world, including China. While there were differences between the major powers in this period, the risk of war was very low, and security competition was muted. This benign geopolitical environment facilitated a globalised economy in which supply chains and interdependence more broadly followed economic incentives without regard for national security risks.

That assumption no longer holds. China and the United States are strategic competitors, and there is a significant risk of war. This fundamentally changed the incentive structure of both nations. In a geopolitical crisis, China would use the leverage it had. The same would be true of the United States. China had been taking concerted steps to reduce its economic and technological exposure to the United

States and to become more self-reliant, but we had not reciprocated. Moreover, China had adopted policies, such as the subsidisation of Chinese industry to force international competitors out of business in strategically important industries, that had a massive and distorting impact on the global economy. Quite apart from the national security risk, China's actions hurt American workers (and those in other countries). There were other drivers behind a shift in policy – the climate change crisis necessitated investments in clean technology, and the public was demanding an approach that directly addressed the daily challenges they encountered.

The administration laid out a new approach to foreign economic policy that aimed to jump-start investment in foundational technologies on the basis that free markets were no longer sufficient given China's non-market practices. It sought to strengthen the resilience of the US economy to external shocks, especially interruptions to supply chains initiated by foreign powers. And it sought to create rules that ensured the global economy worked for ordinary Americans, such as through an agreement on international corporate tax.[37]

The strongest critique of our approach, especially in the Indo-Pacific, was that we had left no room for a free trade component. Asia's large plurilateral free trade agreements are convening platforms that pull countries together and help set the trade rules. We were largely absenting ourselves, or so the critique went. With US tariffs at an average rate of just 2.3 per cent, administration officials believed that making free trade agreements the organising principle of US trade policy was a mistake. But it was quite another thing to make no provision for it at all. We said that we were not opposed to trade, and we didn't rule out increased market access in principle. That was true. But it was also true that the US Trade Representative Katherine Tai had little interest in new trade agreements that expanded market access, and Biden was unwilling to go against the unions.[38] It was unfortunate because tailored bilateral agreements could have included increased market access in specific areas (such as digital commerce) that were mutually beneficial while maintaining the administration's other foreign economic policy goals.

TURBULENCE LEADING TO AN INTENSIFICATION OF DIPLOMACY

When thinking about the trajectory of Biden's China policy and how we got there, it is helpful to distinguish between three different phases.

The first phase ran from the beginning of the administration until mid-2022 and was focused on implementing the ideas described above. The administration was wary of a diplomacy trap whereby Beijing pressed Washington to dilute its competitive actions in exchange for dialogues that went nowhere. There was an expectation that the relationship would be difficult. When Jake Sullivan and Antony Blinken met with China's top diplomat, Yang Jiechi and Minister for Foreign Affairs Wang Yi in Anchorage in March 2021, the two sides clashed in front of the cameras. Yang accused Sullivan and Blinken of hypocrisy and condescension while Wang, referring to the imposition of sanctions on Hong Kong entities shortly before the meeting, said, 'This is not supposed to be the way one welcomes his guests.'[39] But, for the most part, the relationship was relatively stable and there were few flashpoints.

That changed in the turbulent second phase, from mid-2022 to April 2023. It began with Speaker Nancy Pelosi's visit to Taiwan in early August 2022, which she took over the objections of the NSC, the commander of US Indo-Pacific Command Admiral John Aquilino, and others. That trip sparked a furious Chinese reaction. Beijing undertook unprecedented military exercises rehearsing an invasion, sent warplanes and warships across the median line that had previously been tacitly acknowledged as a maritime boundary, and launched ballistic missiles near Taiwan. In October 2022, the administration set out its first tranche of export controls. Then, in late January to early February 2023, we had the balloon incident. And in February and March 2023, the United States and Europe clashed with China over Beijing's provision of lethal assistance to Moscow for its war in Ukraine. Clearly, the relationship was becoming unstable.

This set the stage for the third phase – a dual track strategy of intensified diplomacy and competitive actions. During the clash over lethal assistance to Russia, President Biden gave guidance that he wanted to take the decibel level down a notch or two and open new avenues for dialogue with China. It was easier said than done. Xi had surrounded himself with a tight circle of men whom he had known for decades. They did not talk with Westerners and did not have much of a track record on geopolitics. However, one avenue was the director for the Chinese Communist Party's Central Committee Foreign Affairs Commission, a position initially held by Yang Jiechi and then by Wang Yi, who was also foreign minister. Jake Sullivan would meet with Wang on five occasions. These meetings would often last for two days in places like Geneva, Malta, and Singapore.

The stated purpose of this channel was not to convert China or to find areas of cooperation. It was to have a dialogue in which each side would explain its position in the expectation that this would inject some stability into the relationship and reduce the risk of surprises and misunderstandings that could spiral out of control. Although not its stated objective, the channel did succeed in creating some space for limited and targeted cooperation, such as an agreement to ensure that artificial intelligence models did not have a role in the command and control of nuclear weapons.

Dialogue with Beijing was just one of two tracks of the Biden administration's China strategy. The other was competitive action, defined as steps we needed to take to give the United States a long-term strategic advantage over China, which continued and even intensified in this period. This included expanding and tightening export controls, public listing of Chinese entities responsible for circumventing those controls, actions against agents of the People's Republic of China involved in transnational oppression, and sanctions against Chinese banks involved with Russia. Of the 145 competitive actions taken during the administration, 47 occurred up until May 2023, while 98 took place after, meaning that there was a greater intensity of competitive actions during the period of Sullivan–Wang diplomacy than before.[40]

By the end of the Biden administration, the United States and China each had basically the same strategy towards the other – they were both trying to stabilise the relationship to buy time to prepare for a confrontation or war that each hoped to be able to deter. This was important for us to understand and internalise because it meant that the newfound stability in the relationship was temporary and fragile. It also meant that we needed to use that period of stability to strengthen our position – with investments, resilience, and military modernisation at home, and through alliance-building and competitive actions internationally.

LESSONS LEARNED FROM BIDEN'S CHINA POLICY

Biden's China policy broke new ground on domestic investments in national power, the deepening of alliances, technological export controls, and a realistic diplomatic channel to manage tensions. It did not go as far as some hawks would have liked. For some, we should have reduced our involvement in the crises in Europe and the Middle East to direct more resources (time and attention as well as military assets) to the Indo-Pacific. Others felt that we could have pressed China harder in public, using their missteps with other countries to capitalise on an advantage. And, as mentioned above, our inability to integrate market access into our economic relations with regional actors was a perennial sore point with allies and partners.

Where does the Democratic approach on China go from here? Former Biden officials have written articles that shed some light on this question.

One theme is that the deepening of alliances must evolve to include an integration of manufacturing and production, especially in defence and technology, to keep abreast of China, given that it has a scale advantage over the United States. In an influential article, former Biden officials Kurt Campbell and Rush Doshi wrote:

> Throughout the 20th century, America outproduced and out-innovated Germany, Japan and the Soviet Union. But China is different. On the metrics that matter most in strategic competition, it has already surpassed the United States.[41]

This includes steel, cars, solar panels and other clean technologies, batteries, critical minerals, and ships. Campbell and Doshi argued:

> America's best hope for matching that lies in maximizing its own strength through alliances. That

means no longer treating US allies as dependents under our protection but as partners in building power jointly by pooling markets, technology, military capability and industrial capacity. Investments in American renewal are necessary but insufficient by themselves.[42]

The same applies to alliance cooperation on the extraction and processing of critical minerals and on working with allies to de-risk from China by building trusted supply chains and increasing resilience to economic coercion.

In future Democratic administrations, we can also expect to see other new US initiatives to deepen alliances and partnerships in dramatic ways. In May 2025, Ely Ratner, who served as assistant secretary of defence for Indo-Pacific security affairs in the Biden administration, wrote that the 'time has come for the United States to build a collective defense pact in Asia'. Previously, this type of initiative was 'neither possible nor necessary', but today, in light of a growing threat from China, it is 'viable and essential'. For Ratner, this pact would include the United States, Australia, Japan, and the Philippines with others to join as conditions warrant.[43] Such an initiative would meet with strong Chinese opposition and some US allies might be hesitant, but others may welcome it. Along similar lines, Campbell and Jake Sullivan wrote a piece for *Foreign Affairs* in September 2025 in which they argued that the shortcomings of the partnership model for the United States and India had become clear with the end of the post-Cold War era. They made a case for a treaty alliance with New Delhi, though not based on mutual defence like most US alliances. Instead, a US–India alliance would be 'based on a series of mutual commitments regarding technology, defence, supply chains, intelligence, and global problem solving'.[44]

As we shall see in the next chapter, Trump has moved away from Biden's policy of using technology export controls to help win the AI race. In response, Democrats have doubled down and feel even more ownership over the issue. They are likely to make the national security dimensions of new technologies a key point of differentiation with Republicans and, if they come back to power, they will make this a central part of their China policy. It's hard to know if there will be a return to Biden's export control regime since the technological situation may have changed significantly by then, but the intention and impulse are there. The scope is also there to develop and expand industrial policy to go beyond chips and critical minerals to robotics, connected vehicles, batteries, biotech, and other areas where China has developed advantages over the United States.

Finally, Democrats believe that to compete with China globally, the United States has to have an affirmative offering for countries in the Global South, especially on investment, to provide an alternative to China's Belt and Road Initiative. And it must lead in the provision of global public goods, including on health, the environment, and technology. Less has been written on this issue since the end of the administration, but we can expect it to receive more attention in the coming years.

CHAPTER THREE

Trump comes back

TRUMP BEING TRUMP

In January 2016, as Iowan voters prepared to cast their ballots in the first contest of the presidential primary, the general take on Donald Trump's foreign policy in media and political circles was that he was the ultimate opportunist. He had no fixed opinion on world events and would change his position to whatever worked to his immediate advantage. I began to dig online and found a treasure trove – interviews with Oprah Winfrey and *Playboy* magazine, along with a full-page advertisement he had placed in three national newspapers in 1987.

These records showed that Trump had a remarkably consistent set of visceral beliefs. He felt that America's allies were ripping the United States off. He believed that some of them – Kuwait and South

Korea, for example – should pay a percentage of their wealth for security commitments. He objected to free trade agreements and wanted Washington to use tariffs to negotiate more favourable arrangements. And he had a consistently expressed admiration for strongmen, once praising the Chinese crackdown in Tiananmen Square and dismissing Soviet leader Mikhail Gorbachev as weak for not following suit.

I wrote a piece for *Politico* magazine titled 'Donald Trump's 19th Century Worldview' (and later in 2016, a paper for the Lowy Institute that fleshed out the thesis).[45] I was a little anxious that it would be published before the Iowa caucus because Trump might drop out afterwards. Little did I know that it would still be highly relevant ten years later. There have been many twists and turns and much bureaucratic intrigue in Trump's foreign policy, but this core set of beliefs remains unchanged.

In his first term, Trump's pursuit of these beliefs was constrained by his inexperience and by the so-called 'axis of adults' (advisers such as Gary Cohn, Steven Mnuchin, Mike Pompeo, John Bolton, HR McMaster, and others) who tried to limit the options he was presented with and to inject some stability into his foreign policy. To take one example, in 2017, White House chief economic adviser Gary Cohn took a draft letter terminating a free trade agreement with South Korea off the president's desk to prevent him from signing it. According to Bob Woodward, Cohn was 'appalled' that Trump would pull out of the agreement and told an associate, 'I stole it off his desk . . . I wouldn't let him see it. He's never going to see that document. Got to protect the country.'[46] A similar pattern played out on Trump's policy towards Russia, the US troop presence in South Korea, and other issues.

In his second term, Trump chose officials who would follow his preferences and obey his whims unquestioningly. These ultraloyalists owed their position solely to Trump, had no independent power base and very little experience – Pete Hegseth, who was a presenter on Fox News, Kash Patel, who had been a staffer on Capitol Hill and served in mid-level positions in Trump's first term, and Tulsi Gabbard, who was on the fringes of the Democratic Party, are good examples. Secretary of State Marco Rubio was an exception, but he was at pains to demonstrate his loyalty to Trump and his agenda. This would be an administration where Trump called the shots.

Trump was clear that this time would be substantively different. Much to Danish and European consternation, he said he wanted to acquire Greenland 'for national security reasons'. He also wanted to take back the Panama Canal and routinely mocked Canada's prime minister Justin Trudeau, saying that he wanted to make Canada America's 51st state. Trump began to talk more about emulating President William McKinley, the last president to expand the territory of the United States and a strong supporter of tariffs.[47]

At the working level of the administration, things were also different. Célia Belin, Majda Ruge, and Jeremy Shapiro of the European Council on Foreign Relations wrote a prescient piece in June 2024 that identified three tribes within the America First ecosystem: 'restrainers who want US foreign policy to focus on America; prioritisers who want it to focus on Asia; and primacists who want it to continue to focus globally.'[48] The restrainers included Vice President Vance, the prioritisers Under Secretary of Defence for Policy Elbridge Colby, and the primacists Mike Waltz, who served as Trump's national security adviser and is now his ambassador to the United Nations.

During the transition, the restrainers gained control of the Presidential Personnel Office under Sergio Gor, and they began to place people of that view, or prioritisers, in key positions, especially in the Pentagon, shutting out most of the primacists. However, as each of these factions acknowledged,

President Trump was largely ignorant of these debates and did his own thing. They were competing with each other to win his ear and to dominate day-to-day policymaking at the working level. But all would be caught off guard by the president, who was prone to leaning heavily into one option only to sharply turn into another, as evidenced by his shift from support for diplomacy with Iran to striking its Fordow nuclear facility.

Trump's second term is significant for world order in two ways. One is that Trump's actions could have an enduring international impact. Imagine, for example, if tariffs triggered a global recession or, conversely, if they produced significant domestic revenue with little economic instability. Or, if the decision to pull back from supporting Ukraine caused a Russian victory that then put NATO's Eastern flank under increased pressure. Any of these developments would shape world order in profound ways.

The second impact is that, regardless of the effects of Trump's policies in the immediate future, we are seeing the emergence of a new model for America's role in the world that is likely to be championed by Republicans for some time to come. In this way, it is distinct from Trump's first term, when most of the people around him, including Vice President

Mike Pence, were traditional internationalist Republicans. Occasionally, this model is also distinct from what Trump himself is doing when driven more by personal vanity and pique. In this chapter and the next, I will try to identify the direction of the America First movement after Trump.

All of this – Trump's worldview, the significance of his personnel picks, his determination to bend the world to his will, and the changing nature of the Republican Party – was vividly on view in his foreign economic policy and declaration of a trade war.

LAUNCHING A TRADE WAR

Trump was clear during the campaign that if he returned as president, tariffs would be a central part of his policy. In his inaugural address, he said, 'I will immediately begin the overhaul of our trade system to protect American workers and families. Instead of taxing our citizens to enrich other countries, we will tariff and tax foreign countries to enrich our citizens.'[49] Within his first couple of months, Trump issued an executive order declaring that foreign trade abuses pose a national emergency, which allowed him to authorise aggressive tariffs and investment restrictions.[50] The push for tariffs came to a head on 2 April 2025, which the Trump administration called Liberation Day. Trump laid out a 10 per cent baseline global tariff and then added additional tariffs on top of that. He called them reciprocal tariffs, but the formula was just to calculate the US trade deficit with a given country divided by US imports to that country, and then dividing that number by two. *The Economist* described the formula as being 'almost as random as taxing you on the number of vowels in your name'.[51]

In his remarks announcing the tariffs, Trump fleshed out the case for them and took on the main critique – that tariffs drive global economic instability and recession. He argued that tariffs drove the US economy in the late 19th century, but:

> Then in 1913, for reasons unknown to mankind, they established the income tax so that citizens, rather than foreign countries, would start paying the money necessary to run our government. Then in 1929, it all came to a very abrupt end with the Great Depression, and it would have never happened if they had stayed with the tariff policy. It would have been a much different story. They tried to bring back tariffs to save our country, but it was gone, it was gone, it was too late. Nothing could have been done. It took years and years to get out of that depression, far longer than even FDR – had that office right over there for a long period of time.[52]

This was a bizarre misreading of history but it showed how deeply committed Trump is to tariffs and how he has rationalised their role historically.

The market response was ferocious. US stock indices lost between 9 per cent and 11 per cent of their value within 48 hours of the Liberation Day announcements. The bond markets got jittery as Japanese investors led the exit from US treasuries. According to *The New York Times*, Trump told Congressional Republicans, 'I know what the hell I'm doing', but the White House was nervous of a spiral that could cause a new financial crisis.[53] Trump then announced a 90-day pause on additional tariffs for most countries (China was an exception) while keeping a 10 per cent base rate in place. Afterwards, senior Trump officials claimed this was the plan all along, but the president himself said:

> I was watching the bond market. The bond market is very tricky, I was watching it. But if you look at it now it's beautiful. The bond market right now is beautiful . . . I saw last night where people were getting a little queasy.[54]

Subsequently, the Trump administration negotiated deals with the United Kingdom, Pakistan, Vietnam, Japan, and the European Union. It was clear that Trump intended to deploy the tariffs for his own personal preferences – whether that was to protect Jair Bolsonaro in Brazil or to punish Narendra Modi and India. Still, the broader picture was evident: the Budget Lab at Yale University estimated that the overall average effective US tariff rate was 17.9 per cent in November 2025, the highest since 1934. That compares to an average of approximately 2.4 per cent at the end of the Biden administration.[55]

A senior European policymaker later told me that we learned one new thing from this episode. We knew that Trump was committed to tariffs, but the reversals in the aftermath of Liberation Day told us that he is nervous about the bond markets and responsive to them. He is less worried about retaliation by other states (China may be the exception) because they can be intimidated and pushed around, but the bond markets are beyond his control.

Republicans have generally been opposed to tariffs since the Second World War, so embracing them is quite an adjustment. Trump is not the only factor – there has been growing economic populism in both US parties since the financial crisis and China's economic rise. Nevertheless, Trump has been a critical catalyst. Many reasons have been offered by

Trump and his administration for the tariffs – they are a means of negotiating genuinely free trade, they are a revenue stream to partially replace income tax, and they are a way of encouraging manufacturing at home. But at its core is a belief that, given the size of the US market and the other ways nations depend on US security provision, the United States can compel other countries to pay a premium to deal with it. In an interview with *Time*, Trump described the United States as 'a giant, beautiful store, and everybody wants to go shopping there. And on behalf of the American people, I own the store, and I set prices, and I'll say, if you want to shop here, this is what you have to pay.'[56]

Trump's team began to lay out a rationale that could provide the basis for a long-term commitment to the tariff regime among America Firsters. In a speech at the Hudson Institute in April 2025, the then chair of the Council of Economic Advisers, Stephen Miran, talked about how the United States has provided two 'global public goods for the entire world' since the Second World War. The first, he said, is 'a security umbrella which has created the greatest era of peace mankind has ever known'. The second is that 'the US provides the dollar and Treasury securities, reserve assets which make possible the global trading and financial system which has supported the greatest era of prosperity mankind has ever known'.[57]

Miran said that both of these public goods are costly to provide and that 'President Trump has made it clear that he will no longer stand for other nations free-riding on our blood, sweat, and tears, whether in national security or trade.' Other nations needed to pay more for these public goods. Miran said they could do that in a number of ways – by accepting US tariffs without retaliation, purchasing more US products, increasing defence-related spending with the United States, investing in US manufacturing, or by making direct financial contributions to the US Treasury.

This is an extraordinary shift in US strategy. In an essay in *Foreign Affairs*, Adam Posen of the Peterson Institute wrote that these public goods:

> . . . can be thought of, in economic terms, as forms of insurance. The United States collected premiums from the countries that participated in the system it led in a variety of ways, including through its ability to set rules that made the US economy the most attractive one to investors. In return, the societies that bought into the system were freed to expend much less effort on securing their economies against uncertainty, enabling them to pursue the commerce that helped them flourish.

However, particularly in his second term, 'Trump has switched the United States' role from global insurer to extractor of profit. Instead of the insurer securing its clients against external threats, under the new regime, the threat against which insurance is sold comes as much from the insurer as from the global environment.'[58]

This shifting understanding of public goods – the world ought to pay for what the United States provides – is likely to remain a key part of the America First worldview after Trump departs.

GOING WOBBLY ON CHINA

Getting tough on China has been central to Trump's narrative since he ran for president in 2016 because it is key to his economic message, which is that Americans have been left behind because US leaders have been naive about China. In its first term, the Trump administration went after China economically, but it also laid out a doctrine of great power competition in its National Security Strategy and National Defence Strategy. Senior officials, including Vice President Mike Pence and Secretary of State Mike Pompeo, made speeches about how China represented the greatest threat to the United States.[59] However, there has always been a question around Trump's personal commitment to the geopolitical agenda. When Colin Kahl and I were writing our 2021 book on the geopolitical consequences of the Covid pandemic, *Aftershocks*, I spoke with a senior Trump official who told me that many of the actions they wanted to take against China were gummed up in bureaucratic gridlock until the northern spring of 2020, when Trump lost patience with Xi over Covid and gave the hawks permission to move ahead.

The story of Trump's second-term China policy is that he started out with an extremely tough line, especially on trade, but was chastened by China's response and began to move towards a deal and a stabilisation of tensions.

Shortly after he took office, Trump instructed his administration to scrutinise China's compliance with the 2020 Phase One trade deal (which had required large purchases of US goods), to report on persistent trade imbalances, and to move forward with investment restrictions and a 10 per cent tariff on Chinese imports. Beijing retaliated, and the situation quickly escalated over the following couple of months, reaching boiling point on Liberation Day when US tariffs hit 145 per cent. Trump kept those tariffs in place even as he reduced tariffs on allies when those measures produced instability in the bond market.

What happened next came as something of a shock to the Trump administration. China began to restrict its exports to the United States. Initially, the administration was dismissive. US Treasury Secretary Scott Bessent said:

> I think it was a big mistake, this Chinese escalation, because they're playing with a pair of twos. What do we lose by the Chinese raising tariffs on us? We export one-fifth to them of what they export to us, so that is a losing hand for them.[60]

But, as Adam Posen pointed out in another essay in *Foreign Affairs*, Bessent had it exactly backwards – China had escalation dominance because 'the United States gets vital goods from China that cannot be replaced any time soon or made at home at anything less than prohibitive cost'.[61] Soon, the administration realised that the United States would run short of key machine parts for hospitals and air conditioners, with no obvious substitutes.

China also imposed restrictions on critical minerals and rare earth metals which, according to *The Washington Post*, 'provoked deep consternation at high levels of the administration' because they cut off US defence manufacturers and other key industries from materials necessary for production.[62] This merits some elaboration. To its credit, the Trump administration identified US dependence on China in these areas as a vulnerability. It was something we were deeply concerned about, too. According to the US Geological Survey, the United States is either wholly or more than 50 per cent reliant on imports for 40 of the 50 minerals deemed critical to the US economy and its national security.[63] China serves as the primary source for 22 of these, including minerals such as tungsten and graphite that are essential components for the US defence industry.

China's dominance of this sector didn't happen by accident. Over the past two decades, Beijing has invested approximately US$57 billion in mining facilities around the world, establishing a dominant position in global production and processing capabilities.[64] Meanwhile, Chinese companies have benefited from state subsidies and less stringent environmental regulations, allowing them to undercut competitors and distort global markets. Trump made some positive moves to address this challenge, including by building on the Biden administration's investment in domestic mining and processing facilities for minerals such as lithium and graphite. But these efforts would take time. Meanwhile, the United States was exposed to Chinese actions to restrict access to these materials.

The Biden administration deliberately kept its economic actions towards China targeted and limited to convey the message that if Beijing responded by cutting off critical minerals and rare earths, we would have lots of room to escalate. The Trump administration's announcement of a 145 per cent tariff on all Chinese goods was tantamount to declaring a full-scale trade war. The United States effectively fired all the economic weapons in its arsenal at the start without leaving room for further escalation. As a result, Beijing had no incentive to hold back on ramping up its own controls on critical minerals. It targeted rare earth elements, permanent magnets, and processing technologies. To make matters worse, the Trump administration was openly alarmed by China's response thus signalling to Beijing that it had a real point of leverage.

US and Chinese officials met in Geneva in May 2025, reaching an interim agreement committing the United States to lower newly imposed tariffs to 10 per cent for 90 days. That deadline was subsequently extended multiple times. The two countries seemed on track for a trade deal, and possibly a broader agreement, but in October 2025, Beijing established a sweeping regulatory architecture enabling China to curtail exports of rare earths, critical minerals, and other strategic inputs at short notice, creating a major backlash by signalling that access to these materials could be weaponised at any time. A furious Trump threatened to cancel his upcoming meeting with Xi and increase US tariffs and export controls on chips. Against this backdrop, Trump and Xi met on the sidelines of the Asia-Pacific Economic Cooperation (APEC) summit in South Korea in October 2025 and reached a deal. Beijing agreed to suspend its new export controls for one year while Washington committed to pausing implementation of its '50 per cent rule' governing US export controls on Chinese-owned affiliates and to maintain tariffs at current levels while negotiations continued. Both leaders also endorsed a package of small confidence-building steps, including targeted tariff adjustments and renewed agricultural purchase commitments. The two leaders committed to meeting in April 2026 in China.

By the end of 2025, it seemed as if Xi had the measure of Trump. He had fended off the initial tariff onslaught and inflicted real pain on the United States in response. Trump displayed little interest in competing strategically with China and instead prioritised short-term economic dealmaking. Republican China hawks were concerned, but some believed that China's aggressive actions would ultimately pull the Trump administration back towards a competitive strategy. However, the National Security Strategy, released in early December 2025, dealt with China almost entirely through an economic lens and held out hope that the two countries could reach a 'genuinely mutually advantageous economic relationship'. The strategy was widely interpreted as pulling back from strategic competition and prioritising the Western hemisphere and homeland security over the Indo-Pacific.[65]

TECHNOLOGICAL COMPETITION

As we saw in Chapter 2, Biden had put technological competition front and centre in his China policy. The United States invested at home in cutting-edge technologies, especially advanced semiconductor chips, and it imposed export controls and investment restrictions on China. Initially, Trump maintained this approach (indeed, he had taken a competitive stance on technology in his first term) and introduced new controls, most notably on the H20 chip, which had been designed by Nvidia in response to the Biden administration's controls. The Biden team ran out of time to include the chip in their controls, but in April 2025 Trump banned their export to China.

A rebalancing of power followed. As David Sacks – Trump's AI tsar and a sceptic of export controls – consolidated influence, internal support for export controls weakened. Laura Loomer, a right-wing provocateur with direct access to Trump, reportedly played a decisive role in the dismissal of David Feith, an ideological counterweight to Sacks who led the National Security Council's technology directorate.[66] After Mike Waltz was removed as national security adviser, the NSC was weakened further and became a shadow of its former self. Jensen Huang, the CEO of Nvidia, began to make inroads with Trump personally. Soon, the administration began to ease the controls, lifting restrictions on the H20 after Trump met with Huang. Trump also lifted Biden's Diffusion Rule, which restricted the construction of frontier AI data centres overseas, and promised to ease the controls further after he asked Huang for 15 per cent of all Nvidia H20 sales to China.

In December 2025, Trump doubled down on the H20 decision and allowed Nvidia to sell the H200 chip to China, which was six times more powerful, in exchange for the US government receiving 25 per cent of all sales. Trump's H200 decision marked a dramatic reversal not just of the Biden approach but also of the first Trump administration's efforts, both of which had sought to maintain the largest possible lead over China on AI. Republican senators joined their Democratic counterparts to introduce legislation to ban the export of the H200 but it proved futile. Some in the Trump coalition were furious. Former White House chief strategist Steve Bannon, who remains close to Trump, claimed Sacks 'acted as the agent for the Chinese Communist Party', and accused Jensen Huang of being 'the arms merchant'.[67]

The current administration essentially believes in the addiction thesis, which is that easing export controls will hook Chinese companies on American chips and prevent China from developing its own capability. It is a highly questionable assumption. The addiction hypothesis has not worked in other industries where it has been tried. China remains determined to develop its own production capacity regardless of what the United States does. And the easing of controls now might enable China to erase America's lead in the race for more powerful artificial intelligence.

TOWARDS AN AMERICA FIRST AGENDA

The America First movement appears to have fully embraced Trump's worldview on tariffs, as has most of the Republican Party, but it remains more divided on China policy.

On trade, the position is that America should use its economic and security leverage to extract concessions from other countries in ways that go far beyond tariffs. Rather, countries should pay the United States for reasons that vary depending on who is doing the explaining. For some, it is an entrance fee to the US market. For others, it is in exchange for a security alliance. Elements of the Republican Party are wary of this approach but, as long as the costs and consequences are manageable, it is hard to see it being reversed by a new Republican administration in 2029, not least because Vice President Vance is a strong supporter of the position. Things may change if tariffs cause significant inflation or a downturn in the economy, or if the Democratic Party can convince voters that they are a tax paid by Americans, not foreign nations.

China is more complicated in Republican politics. Many Trump administration officials as well as Republican senators and members of Congress are hawkish on China and see it as a strategic threat to the United States. They are reluctant to speak up against the relaxation of export controls or on Taiwan policy because they do not want to criticise the president, but they privately harbour concerns. Looking beyond Trump, it is hard to say if the shift away from strategic competition will stick or if it will make a return. We will come back to this in Chapter 5. The same is true of Trump's position on alliances and partnerships, to which we now turn.

months, Trump's [illegible] countries should pay the United States for reasons that [illegible] doing them a favour. For some, it is an [illegible] matter to the US [illegible]. For others, it is an exchange for a security alliance. Elements of the Republican Party are wary of this approach but, as long as the costs and consequences are manageable, that might be [illegible] being pursued by a new Republican administration in [illegible] Vice President [illegible] strong support for the [illegible] of [illegible] cause significant [illegible] in the economy [illegible] the Democratic Party can [illegible] they [illegible] Americans [illegible] foreign nations.

[illegible] more [illegible] point [illegible] Trump [illegible] as well as Republican senators and members of Congress are hawkish on China and see it as a strategic threat to the United States. They are reluctant to speak up against the [illegible] of [illegible] on [illegible] but they [illegible] the [illegible]. They [illegible] is hard to [illegible] from [illegible] We will [illegible] in Chapter 7. [illegible] of Trump's [illegible] alliances [illegible]

CHAPTER FOUR

Allies and partners under Trump

WHIPLASH IN ASIA

In an essay in *Foreign Affairs* in January 2025, Bilahari Kausikan, one of Singapore's most astute geopolitical analysts and a former head of its foreign ministry, sounded positively sanguine about Donald Trump's return to the presidency. In Asia, he wrote:

> . . . a second Trump administration does not arouse the same strong emotions that it does among many in the West. For these countries, there is far less concern about Trump's autocratic tendencies and contempt for liberal internationalist ideals. The region has long conducted relations with Washington on the basis of common interests rather than common values. Such an approach fits neatly with Trump's transactional foreign policy because it involves balancing mutual

benefits rather than sustaining the liberal international order.[68]

Kausikan did mention that Trump's rhetoric about tariffs was concerning but he held out hope for a pragmatic America that would find a way of working with Asian nations to their mutual advantage.

On 8 April, shortly after the massive tariff announcements of Liberation Day, Singapore's prime minister Lawrence Wong gave a speech in which he declared that 'the era of rules-based globalisation and free trade is over'. 'This,' he said, 'marks a profound turning point. We are entering a new phase in global affairs – one that is more arbitrary, protectionist, and dangerous.' A couple of months earlier, his colleague, Ng Eng Hen, then defence minister, had told a meeting on the margins of the Munich Security Conference that Asian perspectives of the United States had changed from a force of 'moral legitimacy' and a 'liberator' to 'a great disruptor' and 'a landlord seeking rent'.[69]

Singapore's whiplash reflected a broader concern and disorientation in Asia about the second Trump administration which was at odds with Kausikan's sanguinity. Trump was more ideological and extractive than they anticipated from their experience of his first term, especially on trade and economics.

Singapore was not an isolated example. America's allies and partners all struggled with the same set of problems.

Rhetorically, the Trump administration is more comfortable with America's alliances in the Indo-Pacific than in Europe. Among senior officials, there is very little of the harsh and emotional language present in their discussions of how transatlantic allies take advantage of America. Indeed, they have been reassuring about America's intention to lead in the Indo-Pacific and to work with allies and partners. On a visit to the region in March 2025, for example, Secretary of Defence Pete Hegseth promised to 'truly prioritise and shift to this region of the world in a way that is unprecedented' and to work with the Philippines, Japan, South Korea, and Australia to 'establish the deterrence necessary to prevent war'.[70] It was cheap talk but it was still notable given the absence of such feel-good language from US policy towards Europe. A couple of months later, on his second official trip to the region, he told the Shangri-La Dialogue in Singapore, 'America is proud to be back in the Indo-Pacific – and we're here to stay' in what he said was the 'primary theatre' for the United States.[71]

Speeches aside, relations with allies and partners have been choppy. The Trump administration has hit them hard economically and raised doubts about

America's long-term commitment to their security. The allies have responded in roughly the same way, although the particulars diverge. They are working to get the best deal possible from the United States in the near term, they are investing in their own defence capabilities, they are cooperating more closely with each other, and they are trying not to sacrifice too much in their dealings with China. They are hoping to buy time and ride out the storm.

Australia

The Australian government has largely navigated the economic volatility that unsettled other allies and maintained the optics of a positive partnership. While Australia faces the 10 per cent baseline tariff, it has fared better than many peers, largely because the United States already enjoys a significant trade surplus with Canberra – a fact that arguably mitigates the need for any punitive duties at all. An October 2025 meeting between Trump and Prime Minister Anthony Albanese went well (despite Trump's sideswipe at then Australian ambassador to the United States Kevin Rudd following a loaded question from the media). The Australian government secured a critical minerals agreement by pitching Australia as a 'secure supplier' of rare earths to bypass China. Furthermore, despite an early scare sparked by a US

Department of Defence review, the administration reaffirmed its commitment to AUKUS following intense lobbying from Canberra and American supporters of the agreement. The Albanese government is probably a little relieved that Trump is de-emphasising strategic competition with China and now, post-Liberation Day, is focused more on stabilising the relationship with Beijing.

That said, the overall state of the relationship is strained. The Trump administration has put Australia under considerable pressure to increase its defence spending to 3.5 per cent of GDP (Australia currently spends 2 per cent). According to the *Financial Times*, Elbridge Colby, US under secretary of defence for policy, pressed Japan and Australia to make clear what role they would play if the United States and China went to war over Taiwan.[72] This frustrated the allies since the United States is itself deliberately ambiguous about its plans in that contingency.

The gap in worldviews between the United States and Australia has also grown under the Trump administration, including on climate change and the Middle East. Polling by the Lowy Institute confirms that the Australian public views the US administration with deep scepticism, limiting the government's political room for manoeuvre. The Institute reported that 'Only 36 per cent of the public express any level of trust in America to act responsibly in the world, a 20-point drop since last year and the lowest level on record', while only 25 per cent of Australians expressed confidence in Trump 'to do the right things regarding world affairs'. Despite this, 'the vast majority of Australians (80 per cent) continue to say the alliance is important to Australia's security'.[73]

Australia has sought to mitigate the risks of US unpredictability by continuing its strategy of collective deterrence through deepening ties with its regional partners. This includes the Treaty on Common Security with Indonesia signed in February 2026, which commits the two countries to consult on security matters and consider joint measures if one or both are threatened. During the Biden administration, Canberra also reached agreements with Japan on reciprocal access, India on technology, critical minerals, and supply chains, and South Korea on defence procurement.

Japan

Japan has had a tougher time than Australia. Prime ministers Shigeru Ishiba and Sanae Takaichi have pursued a dual strategy of accommodating US demands where possible while hedging by strengthening ties with other partners. Ishiba was one of the first foreign leaders to meet the newly elected Trump in Washington, in February 2025. The meeting went well, with Trump praising Japan and underscoring the importance of the alliance, which only heightened the shock of the tariffs that followed in March and April. Trump used these tariffs as leverage to negotiate a lopsided trade deal and a punitive investment agreement whereby Japan would invest US$550 billion into the US economy with 90 per cent of the profit after the principal has been repaid going to the United States.[74] The economic tensions had a pronounced impact on public opinion. A poll conducted in June by the *Yomiuri Shimbun*, Japan's largest national daily newspaper, found that a record low 22 per cent of Japanese respondents somewhat or greatly trust the United States.[75]

Washington also pressed Japan on defence spending, which reportedly resulted in Tokyo scrapping the annual 'two-plus-two' security talks between the foreign and defence ministers of both countries because it was irritated by US demands.[76] In mid-November 2025, shortly after Takaichi became prime minister, she publicly warned that a Chinese attack on Taiwan could trigger Japanese military action. This prompted a ferocious Chinese response, including trade boycotts and strident denunciations (China's Consul General in Osaka said that Takaichi's 'filthy head' would be 'cut off').[77] Trump stayed quiet during this feud and he reportedly called Takaichi after a phone call with Xi Jinping to ask her to tone down the rhetoric on Taiwan.[78] Japan subsequently denied this report, although author interviews suggest that something was communicated to Tokyo on this issue.

Despite Trump's enthusiastic endorsement of Takaichi in the lead-up to her landslide re-election in February 2026, Japan is still quietly improving ties with like-minded countries in response to ongoing uncertainty about the US administration.[79] Tokyo has continued to bolster relations with South Korea (maintaining intelligence sharing and trilateral coordination), signed new security and access agreements with the Philippines and Australia, and expanded defence-industrial cooperation with India. At the same time, Tokyo has worked with the European Union and through the G7 to uphold a rules-based economic order and coordinate on economic security, partly to offset US unilateralism on trade. These moves build a dense network of like-minded partners around Japan so that its security and influence don't depend solely on the United States.

South Korea

US–South Korea relations had a slow start in Trump's second term due to the political turmoil in Seoul following the impeachment of Yoon Suk Yeol and the election of a new government under Lee Jae Myung. Once Lee became president, his focus shifted to negotiating a trade deal to reduce the 25 pr cent tariff Trump had imposed in July 2025. A key part of this negotiation was a one-sided US$350 billion investment package similar to the US–Japan deal, but much riskier for Seoul. At one point, Trump even demanded that the entire sum be paid upfront in cash, raising fears inside the South Korean government that meeting such a request would deplete its foreign exchange reserves and trigger a financial crisis.[80] After weeks of tense talks, the two sides agreed on a structure that limited the cash component to US$20 billion annually, with the remainder delivered through phased project-based and shipbuilding investments.

This framework was formally announced during Trump's visit to South Korea for the APEC summit in October. Relations had been troubled earlier in the year by a US Immigration and Customs Enforcement raid in Georgia that resulted in the arrest of more than 300 South Korean nationals constructing a Hyundai battery plant, which deeply angered Koreans.[81] Nevertheless, President Lee awarded Trump the country's highest state honour and presented him with a replica of a historic golden ceremonial crown. Trump declared that he had given South Korea approval to pursue a nuclear-powered submarine program, a major shift in alliance defence policy even though the details are still unclear. Seoul remains nervous about Trump's policy towards North Korea and any drawdown of US forces on the peninsula. Author interviews suggest that the US military and some officials within the administration are acutely aware that the North Korean threat is growing due to the assistance Kim Jong Un is receiving from Russia, but it is never raised publicly. North Korea was not mentioned in the National Security Strategy or in Under Secretary Elbridge Colby's keynote speech at the Sejong Institute on a visit to South Korea in January 2026.[82]

Southeast Asia

The Trump administration has been relatively neglectful of Southeast Asia, which gained no reprieve from the tariffs despite its strategic importance. Vietnam is an instructive example. It benefited from a surge in foreign direct investment that started in Trump's first term (growing from US$15.8 billion in 2016 to US$38.2 billion in 2024), as companies diversified away from China. However, the resulting jump in exports to the United States left Vietnam with the third-largest trade deficit with the

United States, after China and Mexico.[83] It was walloped on Liberation Day with tariffs of 46 per cent. A subsequent agreement reduced the rate to 20 per cent but the economic cost was a clear message to the region – it would need to pay to access the US market.[84] Singaporean professors Yuen Foong Khong and Joseph Chinyong Liow wrote in *Foreign Affairs* that 'Southeast Asian countries may insist that they are staying above the fray, but their policies reveal otherwise. The region is drifting toward China.' They warned that the second Trump administration 'may make Beijing's task easier' if it sticks with its aggressive tariff agenda . . . If it doesn't change its ways, the Trump administration will freely cede the trust and goodwill that its predecessors have built up in Southeast Asia over the past half century.'[85]

Taiwan

The Trump administration's Taiwan policy has been something of a contradiction. Senior administration strategists such as Elbridge Colby have argued that China is the primary long-term threat to the United States and that Washington must deter a Chinese assault on Taiwan. This means larger arms sales, joint training to raise the cost of invasion, and a massive increase in Taiwan's defence spending. Trump's priority, by contrast, is to strike a deal with Beijing, and he is reluctant to do anything on Taiwan that might jeopardise preparations for it.

In July 2025, the *Financial Times* reported that the White House had blocked Taiwanese president Lai Ching-te's transit stop in New York and cancelled a meeting between Taiwan's defence minister Wellington Koo and US officials because Trump feared they might derail US–China trade negotiations.[86] In May 2025, Reuters reported that US officials expected arms sales to Taiwan in Trump's second term to exceed the US$18.3 billion sold in his first term.[87] However, Trump declined to approve a US$400 million military aid package – comprising of munitions and drones – in September 2025.[88] The administration justified the pause by arguing that Taiwan should purchase weapons rather than receive aid and that approving the package might upset trade negotiations. However, by the end of 2025, the Trump administration had gone all-in on arms sales to Taiwan. It initially approved sales worth US$330 million, which comprised aircraft parts including for fighter jets, but followed it up in December with a record-setting US$11 billion arms package. This included HIMARS rocket systems, howitzers, Javelin anti-tank missiles, and drones.[89] At the time of writing, it was unclear if Taiwan's parliament would authorise the funds for the arms purchase, and President Trump told the media he was talking with Xi about whether to go ahead with the arms sales.

Taiwan's dominance of the semiconductor industry through the Taiwan Semiconductor Manufacturing Company (TSMC) has also had an impact on Trump's approach. TSMC produces more than two-thirds of global semiconductor output and more than 90 per cent of leading-edge chips. Trump has publicly complained that Taiwan 'stole' the American semiconductor industry and he frequently threatened tariffs of up to 100 per cent on imported semiconductors. In March 2025, he invited the CEO of TSMC, CC Wei, to the White House to announce a US$100 billion TSMC investment plan to build five new US factories. Trump said, 'We must be able to build the chips and semiconductors that we need right here . . . It's a matter of national security for us.'[90] In truth, construction will take many years, but Trump's comments on dependency suggest he understands that the United States has a clear national interest in preserving the status quo on Taiwan, and therefore in deterring a Chinese invasion.

SOUTH ASIA

Trump had a good relationship with Indian prime minister Narendra Modi in his first term – Modi even attended one of his rallies in Texas in 2019 – and initially the two countries seemed on track to deepen their cooperation in 2025. Modi was an early visitor to the Oval Office in mid-February, and the two leaders issued a joint statement outlining 33 areas where they would work to increase co-operation.[91] JD Vance visited India in April and told his audience, 'if India and the United States work together successfully, we are going to see a 21st century that is prosperous and peaceful. But I also believe that if we fail to work together successfully, the 21st century could be a very dark time for all of humanity.'[92] At the end of April, Scott Bessent told broadcaster CNBC, 'I would guess that India would be one of the first trade deals we would sign.'[93]

On 22 April, the same day that Vance gave his speech, militants killed 26 tourists near Pahalgam in Kashmir.[94] The Indian government blamed Pakistan for the terror attack, and on 7 May it launched strikes against terrorist camps in Pakistan. Pakistan retaliated and tensions steadily increased, with both sides conducting drone and missile strikes. Vance and Secretary of State Marco Rubio made calls to both sides. On the evening of 10 May, the fourth day of fighting, a media conference was called in Delhi to announce a ceasefire, but just before it was about to begin, Trump posted on his social media platform

Truth Social, 'After a long night of talks mediated by the United States, I am pleased to announce that India and Pakistan have agreed to a FULL AND IMMEDIATE CEASEFIRE.'[95] New Delhi insists that Kashmir is a purely bilateral issue and it rejects any attempt at international mediation, so it denied that Trump had anything to do with the negotiations.

Trump and Modi spoke by phone on 17 June. According to *The New York Times*, Trump told Modi how proud he was of bringing the India–Pakistan conflict to an end and said that Pakistan was nominating him for the Nobel Peace Prize, implying that Modi should do the same. Modi was agitated and told Trump that the United States had nothing to do with the ceasefire. It had been settled bilaterally.[96] In the weeks following, the relationship began to deteriorate. A trade deal was reportedly on the table but Trump rejected it, demanding additional concessions on US agricultural and dairy exports to India that Modi was unwilling to give. Trump imposed a 25 per cent tariff on India and would later impose an additional 25 per cent to punish India for its oil trade with Russia. Peter Navarro, a senior White House official, would routinely lambast India in comments to the media.

Meanwhile, Pakistan won favour with the Trump administration.[97] Back in March, it had arrested an Islamic State leader who had allegedly orchestrated the 2021 Abbey Gate bombing in Kabul, Afghanistan, that killed 13 US troops. In an address to Congress, Trump thanked Pakistan 'for helping arrest this monster'.[98] A few months later, the president hosted the country's army chief, Asim Munir, for lunch, a highly unusual move that Pakistani officials believe thawed relations.[99]

Unlike India, Islamabad has credited Trump with negotiating the ceasefire in Kashmir, and praised him for it. The country has also offered itself as a hub for bitcoin mining and a source of rare earth metals, both issues of high interest to the administration and Trump personally. Pakistani leaders endorsed a partnership between the country's crypto council and World Liberty Financial, the crypto firm co-founded by Trump's sons. In July, these overtures appeared to pay off: Trump agreed to a trade deal with Pakistan that reduced the tariff rate from 29 per cent to 19 per cent, which at the time was less than half the rate currently imposed on India.

Trump's embrace of Pakistan belies the growing problems it poses for America. In late 2024, then President Biden's deputy national security adviser Jon Finer, drawing on declassified US intelligence, said Pakistan was developing a long-range ballistic missile that could eventually allow the country to target the continental United States with nuclear weapons (Pakistan called the US assessment 'unfounded'). The Biden administration had earlier sanctioned a state-owned entity allegedly involved in the program.[100] The Trump administration, by contrast, has said nothing about it.

There has been bipartisan support for deepening cooperation with India for more than a quarter of a century. This cooperation accelerated after the 2020 border skirmish between Indian and Chinese military forces. This is now in jeopardy. There has been a significant backlash in Indian politics against the United States after Trump's efforts to insert himself into India–Pakistan relations and his subsequent imposition of punitive tariffs. In response, Modi visited Russia, underscoring his close ties to Putin, and participated in a Shanghai Cooperation Organisation summit in China. There is little risk that India will align with China – a geopolitical impossibility given the rivalry stemming from the 2020 border clash and Delhi's worries about Beijing's intentions – but it is possible that US–India relations will atrophy and stall. There were some indicators in late 2025 and early 2026 that tensions were easing. Modi and Trump exchanged positive public messages, and the two countries made some progress towards a trade deal. On 2 February 2026, Trump and Modi announced a deal that cut US tariffs to 18 per cent in exchange for India halting purchases of Russian oil and reducing its trade barriers.

The shift away from India and towards Pakistan appears to be more a function of Trump's personality and temperament than a pronounced shift among America Firsters. Vance, Bessent, and other officials appear sympathetic to India and supportive of a closer partnership, although they are not willing to challenge Trump on this point. However, even if the hostility towards India is not widely shared in the administration, it could still have a deleterious effect on the relationship.

WESTERN HEMISPHERE

In his second term, Donald Trump abandoned the idea that the Western Hemisphere is mainly a community of democracies bound together by shared values and economic integration. He viewed the Monroe Doctrine – a foundational US foreign policy stating that European powers should not colonise the newly independent nations of the Americas – not as a warning to external powers to stay out but as a claim of ownership over the internal affairs of the hemisphere. To Trump, Latin America and Canada are not partners; they are a security buffer to be fortified and a resource zone to be exploited.

This 19th-century worldview was evident early in 2025 when Trump, in a speech that many initially dismissed as bluster, declared that the United States would take back the Panama Canal, calling the 1977 Torrijos–Carter Treaties a 'foolish gift' that had allowed China to gain a foothold in the Americas.[101] While no military action was taken to seize the canal, the rhetoric signalled a shift towards a more coercive approach.

Trump's designation of Mexican drug cartels as Foreign Terrorist Organisations in early 2025 fundamentally changed the legal and military landscape. It allowed the administration to threaten kinetic strikes – drone and missile attacks – against cartel infrastructure on Mexican soil. When Mexico's president Claudia Sheinbaum called these threats 'slanderous' and a violation of sovereignty, Trump responded with tariffs designed to force Mexico into compliance with his demands regarding drug interdiction and migration control.

To the north, the shock was even more profound. When Canadian prime minister Justin Trudeau pushed back against 25 per cent tariffs on Canadian steel and aluminium, Trump openly mocked him, joking to a room of governors in February that perhaps Canada would be better off as America's '51st state' to avoid the duties. He repeatedly called

Trudeau 'Governor' and pressed for Canada to join the United States. In March 2025, Canada elected Mark Carney on a platform of Canadian independence and it began to hedge against Trump's pressure.

Further south, Trump replaced a policy of regional engagement with one of ideological patronage. He embraced Argentina's libertarian president Javier Milei, offering him preferential investment deals, a currency swap to ease his government's fiscal pressures, and political support. Conversely, he undermined left-leaning governments such as Lula's in Brazil (where he embraced the pro-Bolsonaro opposition) and Gustavo Petro's in Colombia.

This approach reached a dangerous peak with Venezuela. Trump ramped up sanctions and authorised limited strikes on Venezuelan maritime assets, ostensibly to stop drug trafficking but clearly intended to signal toughness. This culminated in an unprecedented military operation on 3 January 2026, when US forces successfully launched a large-scale raid to capture Venezuelan president Nicolás Maduro and transfer him to New York to face longstanding US narco-trafficking and narco-terrorism charges. Trump publicly declared that the United States would 'run' Venezuela during a transition period and promised to use the country's oil resources to serve

American interests. His administration also sought to work with the Venezuelan vice president Delcy Rodríguez rather than recognise the winner of the last election, opposition figure Edmundo González. At the time of writing (mid-February 2026), the path forward for Venezuela remained entirely unclear. But the episode underscored Trump's desire to dominate the Western Hemisphere.

The ultimate consequence of this strategy is a fractured region. By demanding loyalty without offering mutually beneficial economic development, and by using economic coercion against partners, Trump has created a vacuum. While his administration talks tough on China globally, his tactics have arguably made Beijing an even more attractive economic partner for nations desperate to diversify away from an unpredictable and hostile Washington. For example, Lula spoke about seeking an indestructible relationship with China while Brazil significantly increased its agricultural exports there; Colombia joined the Belt and Road Initiative in 2025; and Peru is consolidating its position as the hub for China–South America trade. Even the pro-Trump president of Argentina, Javier Milei, had abandoned his tough-on-China rhetoric and was planning a visit to Beijing in 2026 to improve trading links between the two countries. Canadian prime minister Mark Carney made a trip to Beijing in January 2026 and agreed to a set of measures to reset and expand economic ties, including significant tariff reductions on Canadian agricultural products and Chinese electric vehicles.

RUSSIA AND EUROPE

In February 2025, Vice President JD Vance went to the Munich Security Conference and gave a speech admonishing America's European allies: 'the threat that I worry the most about vis-à-vis Europe is not Russia, it's not China, it's not any other external actor . . . what I worry about is the threat from within, the retreat of Europe from some of its most fundamental values.'[102] He was referring to actions against far-right parties such as the Alternative for Germany (Afd) and efforts to stop Russian disinformation. During Vance's speech, German defence minister Boris Pistorius sat in the second row of the audience, clearly upset and calling out, 'That is unacceptable.' In remarks afterwards, he rejected the vice president's characterisation of European governance and said 'democracy must be able to defend itself against the extremists who want to destroy it'.[103]

Vance's speech shocked Europeans, but it was indicative of a broader shift from the first Trump administration to the second. In his first term, Trump admonished European allies for not spending enough on defence. He also reached out to Putin, most notably at the Helsinki summit. But Trump was always hemmed in by his own team. This time around, his team had a much more pronounced anti-European tinge. This was evident in March 2025 when details of the Trump cabinet's Signal chat on striking Yemen leaked to *The Atlantic*. Vance raised some concerns with the strikes, suggesting that Europe had the most to gain: 'I just hate bailing Europe out again.' US Secretary of Defence Pete Hegseth replied, 'I fully share your loathing of European free-loading. It's PATHETIC.'[104] It further underscored the Trump team's antagonism towards the NATO alliance.

The point of greatest tension between the Trump administration and Europe is Ukraine. Europe and the Biden administration both saw the outcome of the Russia–Ukraine war as vital to Europe's future security and, by extension, to the transatlantic alliance. A victory for Russia could embolden it and create a geopolitical black hole at the heart of Europe, destabilising it in myriad ways. Trump, by contrast, felt the United States had no stake in the outcome and, if anything, the war was an obstacle to his goal of rebuilding ties with Russia. After the 2024 presidential election, his team clearly believed that if they offered Putin a freezing of territorial lines and no Ukrainian membership of NATO, the war would come to an end. During the transition of administrations, we told the Trump team that we were confident such a deal would not be enough for the Russians. Putin wanted more – more territory and, crucially, a cap on the size of the Ukrainian military. He wanted a neutered Ukraine, not a neutral Ukraine. But the advice went unheeded. The Trump team would need to figure it out on its own.

First, though, Trump would try to strongarm Ukraine into making a deal. In the showdown with President Volodymyr Zelenskyy in the Oval Office on 28 February 2025, he told the Ukrainian leader he was gambling with World War III, and he subsequently suspended US military and intelligence assistance to Ukraine.[105] The public nature and raw emotions of the meeting shocked the Europeans and portended a major shift in US policy. In the weeks following, the United Kingdom, France, and Germany worked hard to repair relations between Kyiv and Washington. They pressed Zelenskyy to stop demanding concessions on security guarantees as a precondition for a ceasefire. Instead, he should call for an immediate and unconditional cessation of violence. The Russians would not agree to such a call, but it would flip the script with Trump. At a meeting with US officials in Jeddah in March,

Ukraine took that step and endorsed an immediate 30-day ceasefire. Relations with the United States were pieced back together and military assistance was restored.

In April, Trump proposed a peace deal far more favourable towards Russia than anything previously proposed or that the Biden administration would have offered. It included US recognition of Russian sovereignty over Crimea, de facto recognition of the territory it occupied elsewhere in Ukraine, a lifting of all sanctions, and enhanced US–Russia economic cooperation. But Moscow effectively rejected it.[106] Russia demanded the full withdrawal of Ukraine from Donetsk, Luhansk, Kherson, and Zaporizhzhia, and recognition of Russia's sovereignty over those oblasts (regions) as well as Crimea. It also wanted severe caps on the strength of the Ukrainian armed forces and the cessation of Western military aid to Ukraine. Such far-reaching demands were more than even the Trump team could accept. In May, Vance told Fox News that the Russians were asking 'too much,' adding that 'Russia can't expect to be given territory that they haven't even conquered yet'.[107]

Ukraine and Russia met for talks in Istanbul in June, but all it revealed was the gap between the two sides.[108] Trump began imposing numerous two-week deadlines for progress, all of which Putin spurned. Zelenskyy and European leaders became more skilled in their diplomacy with the White House. Trump began to blame Putin publicly, albeit somewhat sporadically. In July, for example, Trump told a luncheon meeting with the White House Faith Office, 'We thought we had a deal numerous times. I get home, I'd say, "First Lady, I had the most wonderful talk with Vladimir. I think we're finished." And then I'd turn on the television or she'll say to me one time, "Well that's strange because they just bombed a nursing home."'[109] Trump agreed to sell arms to Europe for transfer to Ukraine, and promised additional pressure on Russia, most likely in the form of sanctions.

Amid rhetoric and rumours of rising pressure, US Special Envoy to the Middle East Steve Witkoff made a trip to Moscow to meet Putin on 6 August. He seems to have left that meeting with the impression that the Russians had made a concession on security guarantees for Ukraine, which could have opened space for a deal. It was agreed that Putin and Trump would meet about a week later in Alaska. The Anchorage summit was shorter than expected and the US side briefed that significant progress had been made – Russia was willing to accept a European security guarantee for Ukraine with an American backstop. This seemed too good to be true, and it was. In the original Russia–Ukraine talks to end the war, held in Istanbul in March 2022, Russia presented a plan for an external security guarantee for Ukraine that would give Moscow an effective veto over whether it was ever invoked. Moscow subsequently confirmed that this was the type of security guarantee it had in mind. A Western guarantee with European troops was out of the question.[110]

In the months that followed, Trump would repeatedly appear to be on the cusp of truly helping Ukraine prevail against Russia only for him to conduct an abrupt about-turn following contact with Putin. At the time of writing, Trump was still attempting to bridge the gap between Russia and Ukraine but Putin was resisting a deal that was heavily tilted in his favour and looked to be sticking to maximalist demands that would be impossible for Ukraine to accept. The National Security Strategy also confirmed that Trump does not see Russia as a security competitor or threat to the United States and is mainly concerned with stabilising the relationship.

Ukraine was not the only point of tension. For Trump, alliance problems have as much to do with economics and trade as with security. He blamed Europe for free-riding on the United States and not spending enough on its own defence. On trade, he said at one point that the 'European Union is, in many ways, nastier than China'.[111] In his first six months, he made progress on both. By the NATO summit in June 2025, European member states had committed to spend more on defence: 3.5 per cent of GDP plus another 1.5 per cent on defence-related infrastructure for a headline rate of 5 per cent.[112] And in July 2025, he secured a trade deal with the European Union that provided for a 15 per cent tariff on most European goods with no reciprocal tariff on US goods into Europe.[113] The deal was manifestly imbalanced but Brussels agreed to it to help preserve the broader transatlantic relationship. The imbalanced tariffs were a price that would be paid to ensure continued US cooperation on Ukraine and other issues.

Perhaps the greatest crisis with Europe occurred in January 2026. Emboldened by his successful raid to capture Nicolás Maduro, Trump revived his interest in Greenland and made it clear that he intended to take control of it from Denmark. He argued that this was the only way the United States could be sure that it would not fall into Russian or Chinese hands, but this was hardly credible. Greenland was protected under the NATO treaty and Denmark had made it clear it was willing to accommodate all of Trump's substantive policy concerns, including stationing more US troops on the island. Copenhagen's only red lines were Denmark's territorial integrity and the right of Greenlanders to self-determination. Nevertheless, Trump insisted on control. 'When we own it, we defend it. You don't defend leases the same way, you have to own it,' he said.

Trump promised to impose tariffs on countries that joined Denmark in a military exercise in Greenland that was intended to demonstrate a collective willingness to do more for Arctic security. Europe responded by promising tariffs of its own and some leaders endorsed the use of the Anti-Coercion Instrument, which was originally developed to respond to Chinese pressure. As tensions rose, Trump went to the World Economic Forum in Davos and appeared to back down, ruling out the use of force for the first time and then accepting a vague framework for cooperation proposed by NATO Secretary General Mark Rutte, which included revisions to the 1951 Defence of Greenland Agreement and cooperation on critical minerals, the Golden Dome missile shield, and Arctic security. All of this had been on offer to Trump before, so why did he finally accept it? A key part of the explanation appears to have been Denmark's unwillingness to compromise on its two red lines. Also, Europe appeared willing to impose real costs on the United States if Trump tried to take control of

Greenland. Finally, there were signs of instability and weakness in the bond market.

By mid-February 2026, transatlantic relations appeared to stabilise. Marco Rubio's speech in Munich was perceived as reassuring by Europeans even though it was just a softer and more supportive way of saying what Vance had said a year earlier. But the Greenland crisis left a real mark. The United States had threatened a steadfast NATO ally.

DOING DEALS WITH AMERICA

The Trump approach to alliances and partnerships assumes that these arrangements are an inherently bad deal for America, and it seeks compensation for the security protection the United States provides. It also presses allies to build up their militaries so the United States can do less. There is a scenario in which the build-up works and the United States has more capable allies, but it is also possible that Trump's approach will fracture the US alliance system and weaken deterrence, thus making a security crisis more likely in the near future. It could also create opportunities for China to outcompete the United States for influence globally. These are themes I examine in the next and final chapter.

CHAPTER FIVE

The world with two Americas

DIVERGENT WORLDVIEWS

America's allies and partners need to prepare for a world in which US strategy shifts dramatically between America First and liberal internationalist approaches from president to president. The contours of each are now coming into focus, although they are still contingent on the Democratic Party's debate on its future foreign policy and what happens in the Republican Party after Trump leaves office.

Democratic foreign policy

The Biden administration was not a monolith, but nevertheless, it is possible to discern a worldview and strategy distinct from its Democratic predecessors, especially the Obama administration. I am setting aside the Middle East here, which I deal with in the next section and is something of a special case.

The first piece of this worldview is that the Biden administration more fully embraced the notion that the United States is engaged in a strategic competition with China and other revisionist authoritarian powers. It sought to invest in America's national power at home and abroad, to build long-term advantage over China, and to manage that competition so it did not spiral into a full-blown confrontation or conflict.

The second is that the Biden administration believed the United States could and should deepen and strengthen its alliances and partnerships, particularly relating to technology and economic security. We saw this especially in the Indo-Pacific with AUKUS, technological cooperation with India, trilateral diplomacy with South Korea and Japan, and a new agreement with the Philippines.

The third was a shift away from unfettered globalisation and support for a new foreign economic framework that included a targeted industrial policy and prioritising problems such as supply chain resilience.

Finally, Biden was more comfortable than his predecessors in either party in helping Ukraine defend itself against Russian aggression. The administration provided vast quantities of weapons, helped Ukraine build its drone program, and provided invaluable intelligence cooperation.

Each of these ideas is likely to endure and shape the foreign policy of a future Democratic administration, but there is an active debate on this and other subjects.

Perhaps the most interesting question is what lessons Democrats will take from Trump's second-term foreign policy. It is still early days, but three potential themes come to mind.

First, Democrats now tend to believe the Republican Party is not going to return to its internationalist past. The Trumpian fever will not break. Anything a Democratic president accomplishes can be fully reversed with the next election. This makes it particularly important for a future Democratic president to act with great urgency to create new realities that may be resilient to fluctuations in American politics. As discussed in Chapter 3, this may mean much deeper integration in the defence and technological industrial bases of allies and partners.[114] It may also mean helping European allies in particular build up their own capabilities so they can act without full US backing in a crisis or conflict.

Second, Democrats have seen how Trump has wielded power assertively towards allies and partners in pursuit of his ideology (tariffs) and personal preferences (helping leaders who agree with him). Some wonder whether a future Democratic administration should borrow a page from his playbook and be more forceful in pushing their agenda. Take technology export controls as an example. The Biden administration crafted an agreement on semiconductor controls with the Netherlands and Japan, but the ensuing compromise meant China had time to stockpile chips before the controls kicked in. Might the threat of tariffs help bring allies on board more quickly? The same could be said for addressing allied overdependency on China for critical minerals.

These Democrats point out that the key difference from the Trump administration is that this power would be exercised to strengthen the team comprised of America's allies and partners and not to exploit them for economic and financial gain. A more assertive approach may be needed to make sufficiently fast progress. Others feel that after Trump, American power is likely to be diminished and that in a multipolar world the United States will have to be more deferential to the views of others. Adopting a more assertive approach could further undermine US influence internationally and make it harder to strengthen alliances.

Third, some Democrats believe they should increase the emphasis on the Western Hemisphere in a future foreign policy, albeit in a very different way to the Trump administration. While the Biden administration made important strides with the Americas Partnership for Economic Prosperity and the Los Angeles Declaration on Migration and Protection, the administration's bandwidth was too often consumed by Covid in its first year and by crisis management in Haiti, Venezuela, and on the southern border later on. There may be an opportunity in a future administration to deepen cooperation on trade, investment, supply chain resiliency, migration, and competing with China. This will likely require a more flexible approach to trade, not just on market access but also on easing Buy America provisions, which inhibited agreements with partners such as Brazil in the Biden administration.

Bidenism looks more likely to shape Democratic foreign policy in the years ahead than Obamaism. With the exception of the Middle East, there is little sign of a full-throated critique by Democrats of the core pillars of Biden's foreign policy. That said, politics can move in unexpected directions. The voter base of the party is dissatisfied with the leadership and it is possible that this could lead to a different foreign policy if an insurgent candidate wins the

2028 primary. There are some early indicators of a debate with progressives in a number of areas.

On China policy, there are those who believe Biden overstated the China threat and was too slow and reluctant to engage in diplomacy with Beijing. Jessica Chen Weiss, an academic who served for a year on the State Department's policy planning staff, wrote a number of articles in which she criticised Biden's China policy for placing too much emphasis on out-competing China and lacking any objective metrics of success or a clear idea of a desired end-state. Others have argued for prioritising areas of cooperation with Beijing and a mutual reduction of tensions.[115]

The defence budget and military modernisation are also likely to be subjects of contention. Biden did not significantly increase the defence budget beyond the rate of inflation, but some of his officials believe he should have. He did make some progress on repairing the defence industrial base, but a more fundamental overhaul is likely required. Then there are those on the left of the party who believe US foreign policy is already overmilitarised and will be inclined to oppose significant budget increases or elements of military modernisation, for instance, of the nuclear arsenal.

There is also a more fundamental disagreement. Those who want to strengthen and modernise the military are genuinely worried that the world is closer to a wider war than at any time since the early 1980s, or maybe even the early 1960s. They are not confident that the United States maintains a qualitative and quantitative edge over its likely adversaries. On the left, there are those who feel this is overstated and worry that a ramped-up US defence budget could feed a militarism that is itself destabilising.

Democrats could also struggle with international economic policy. A number of Democratic-leaning economists were critical of the administration's tilt away from free trade and neoliberalism. Arguably, we saw a return of the more free-market oriented wing of the party in Kamala Harris's 2024 presidential campaign. Nevertheless, it is hard to see a fully fledged return to neoliberalism in a Democratic primary. On the other side of the ledger, Democrats may be divided on what to do about Trump's tariffs. Most of the foreign policy community and economists will be in favour of a negotiated and reciprocal removal, but others may favour keeping them for the revenues or for other reasons.

If a true alternative does not emerge, Democrats are likely to repackage the core elements of Biden's approach as something novel that moves beyond his administration rather than builds on it. In an article in *Foreign Affairs*, Rebecca Lissner and

Mira Rapp-Hooper, both colleagues in the Biden administration, warned that Democrats should not try to restore the old order but should instead adopt 'a "zero based" review of its foreign policy: a clean slate from which to reevaluate and justify its long-held interests, values, and policies'. One of their core ideas is that alliances 'could be recentered on economic and technological cooperation', which is a key Biden policy.[116] Similarly, Senator Elissa Slotkin gave a speech arguing that a future Democratic administration must treat economic security as national security, win the tech race against China, and 'fundamentally rethink how to protect Americans since they are now on the frontlines', especially on cyber and economic security.[117] Again, all policies closely associated with Biden.

All this reflects a basic political reality: Biden is unpopular and blamed for the 2024 election defeat. In rhetoric and age, he represents a bygone era. So the party may pretend to move on even as it likely builds on what he left: strategic competition, deeper alliances and partnerships, a post-neoliberal foreign economic policy, and support for Ukraine.

Republican foreign policy

Trump's second term has seen the emergence of a new generation of Republican policymakers and officials who genuinely believe in the America First creed and want to tear down and remake the international order in fundamental ways. There is widespread agreement among America Firsters that the old international order has not served the United States well and that Americans need to be compensated for the provision of global public goods and security alliances. The definition of the national interest is drawn much more narrowly than in the past, with significant implications for any action perceived to arise out of an enlightened sense of the common good, such as development assistance.

This group is led by Vice President JD Vance, who calls himself part of the 'postliberal' right and has spoken of the rules-based international order as a means to enrich corporate interests at the expense of ordinary Americans.[118] Russ Vought, who became director of the Office of Management and Budget in Trump's second term after also holding the role in the first, told *Politico* in 2024 that Vance and his allies (among whom he included himself) view themselves as defenders of an older form of conservatism that harks back to the conservative populism of the interwar period, when the far right of the Republican Party supported high tariffs and strict limits on immigration, and opposed American involvement in overseas conflicts.[119]

There are some areas where the emerging America First worldview dovetails perfectly with Trump's views and actions, but there are others where it may diverge. This is a little difficult to discern since Vance and others will never directly criticise the president's actions. Similarly, it is challenging to identify areas where other Republicans harbour concerns about Trump's approach and may push to go in another direction after his term ends.

That said, we can identify some contours of a future America First worldview, and areas of debate among Republicans.

There is broad America First support for the tariff regime, mainly as a source of revenue but also as a means of encouraging domestic production. In the days after Liberation Day, there were signs of Republican lawmakers such as Ted Cruz expressing concern about a trade war and the impact on global markets, but that ebbed away as markets rose again. If the economy remains relatively robust through to 2028, support for tariffs will likely stay. If the economy runs into serious difficulties and tariffs are identified as a contributing cause, then there might be more debate. But, all else being equal, the Republican embrace of tariffs is likely to endure.

A throughline in Trump's second-term foreign policy has been his actions to support his preferred political factions in foreign countries: Brazil, Argentina, Hungary, Germany, South Africa, and elsewhere. He has done so with a mix of tariffs, sanctions, financial support, and public diplomacy. This trend could well outlast Trump if Vance is the nominee because he seems fully supportive of it. Someone like Marco Rubio may be more inclined to support centre-right parties and avoid weighing in on the domestic politics of treaty allies, although he would likely be willing to do so for non-allied countries.

Trump has been deeply critical of Europe for not spending more on defence, but at the same time, he seems to be relatively satisfied with promises to increase that spending and is not pressing for an immediate reduction in US force posture. He frequently disparages European politicians but is also prone to flattery and has gone back and forth with European leaders in his second term, with relations fraught but relatively stable before the Greenland crisis of 2026. That, it is important to acknowledge, still has the potential to seriously damage the alliance.

Some America Firsters seem even more hostile to European governments than is Trump himself. This was on display in what Secretary of Defence Pete Hegseth and Vice President JD Vance said in the leaked Signal chat of March 2025. But it can also be gleaned from Vance's speech at the Munich Security

Conference, his comments in February's Oval Office meeting with Ukrainian president Volodymyr Zelenskyy, and other remarks, including as a Senate candidate in 2022 when he said, 'I gotta be honest with you, I don't really care what happens to Ukraine one way or another.'[120] Most notably, the hostility towards Europe was evident in the National Security Strategy, which warned of 'civilizational erasure' in Europe and promised to cultivate 'resistance to Europe's current trajectory in European nations'.[121]

It is entirely possible that a post-Trump America First administration will seek to systematically undo the transatlantic alliance, withdraw from the European theatre, and actively back their political allies in European countries. Here again, Rubio may be an exception, in that he would likely be more concerned by the Russia threat and more convinced of the necessity of a transatlantic alliance, albeit one in which Europe is shouldering more of the burden. In a way, he is using wedge issues such as the revocation of visas and strikes on Venezuela to package a more traditional Republican foreign policy as America First.

The biggest debate in the America First movement post-Trump is likely to be on China and alliances in the Indo-Pacific. In his second term, Trump has downplayed strategic competition, prioritised dealmaking with Beijing, and either neglected or damaged most of America's alliances and partnerships in the region. Much of the conservative establishment, and the America First movement, has a more hawkish perspective on China, seeing it as the most significant strategic threat to the United States. Vance, for instance, has framed the China threat in terms of its impact on everyday Americans but has also described it in geopolitical terms. In 2024, after he was named as Trump's running mate, he said that the main reason they had to bring the Russia–Ukraine war 'to a rapid close [was] so America can focus on the real issue, which is China. That's the biggest threat to our country and we are completely distracted from it.'[122] After Trump, America Firsters are also likely to be more disciplined in their approach to allies and partners in the Indo-Pacific. For instance, it is hard to see other Republican leaders going after India so stridently because of a perceived personal slight from Modi over a nomination for the Nobel Peace Prize or applying tariffs so broadly to countries in Southeast Asia even though it undermines efforts to compete with China for regional influence.

THE MIDDLE EAST

The Middle East does not easily fit into the framework I have presented, in which Biden and Trump have set forward a strategic paradigm that challenges the status quo and is likely to shape the future debate in Washington on policy towards the region.

For the first two-and-a-half years of his administration, Biden's approach to the Middle East was to reduce tensions in the region, restore deterrence against Iran, and promote integration among the region's countries and with external partners. There were some wins to point to – a ceasefire in Yemen, an economic corridor connecting India to Europe through the United Arab Emirates, Saudi Arabia, Jordan, and Israel, and progress in talks for a treaty with Saudi Arabia that would result in normalisation of relations between it and Israel. This is what led senior officials to say that the region was quieter than it had been for many years. That progress was shattered by the Hamas attack on 7 October 2023, which, in my view, was intended to ignite a conflict so large that it would destroy the integration taking place in the region, particularly between Israel and the Gulf Arab states. In the weeks leading up to the attack, we had been worried about events in the West Bank, which seemed like it was on the brink of a crisis. But no one was tracking a threat from Hamas, not least the Israelis, who had left the border largely undefended.

This is not the place for a detailed analysis of the war in Gaza. Many of my colleagues and I are still trying to figure out what could and should have been done differently. There were successes – by the end of the administration, Hamas's leadership in Gaza had been killed, Iran was in the weakest position it had been in since 1979, Hezbollah had been gravely depleted in Lebanon, and Bashar al-Assad was gone as leader of Syria. But every single person in Gaza had been displaced, many civilians had died, and the war continued for much longer than needed. Israeli prime minister Benjamin Netanyahu frequently promised to end the war within a few weeks but always found a reason to keep going, which raised fundamental questions about whether we conveyed our views with adequate resolve and consequence.

In the next three years, Israel, Gaza, and US policies towards the Middle East will be some of the most difficult issues for Democrats to deal with. Debate will be heated, and will likely be between two positions. The first will call for a more normal allied relationship with Israel. The United States should remain supportive and it should sell arms and continue to provide strategic support. Nevertheless, Washington should not be afraid to say when US interests diverge from those of Israel and it should be willing to make this clear to Jerusalem, and to the public, when it happens. The second view is likely to be more critical of any alliance with Israel and to oppose military and strategic cooperation, especially if Netanyahu or anyone further to the right of him is in power.

The Republican position on the Middle East is also difficult to discern, albeit perhaps a little easier than with Democrats. In the first few months of his second term, Trump seemed relatively cool towards Netanyahu. He carried on talks directly with Hamas, negotiated an end to the war with the Houthis on the same day they attacked Ben Gurion airport, and seemed to be pursuing a nuclear deal with Iran that would not meet most of Israel's demands for a halt to uranium enrichment. That all changed with the Israeli attack on Iran in June 2025. We still do not know exactly what happened, but it seems likely that Israel made the decision to attack unilaterally without American support. When the attacks appeared to have generally succeeded and Iranian retaliation was less than expected, and when one important part of the operation remained unfinished and could only be completed by the United States (attacking the Fordow uranium enrichment facility), Trump ordered a US strike. He subsequently declared that the Iranian program had been obliterated and demanded, successfully, that Israel agree to a ceasefire at a time when

Netanyahu seemed to be pressing for regime change in Tehran. At the time of writing, tensions are rising again, with the United States staging a military build-up in the Persian Gulf even as Washington and Tehran negotiate.

Trump's strike on Iran meant that his relations with Israel were generally seen as rock solid, but tensions were clearly bubbling beneath the surface. For example, he was visibly vexed by Israel's September 2025 attack on Hamas's political leadership in Doha, Qatar, and insisted Netanyahu issue an apology. After the ceasefire was agreed, White House officials were vocal when they felt Israel was putting it at risk with an assassination of a top Hamas commander.[123] Some America Firsters appear to be sceptical of a close alignment with Netanyahu's foreign policy and are reluctant to get involved in more wars in the Middle East, as attested by Vice President Vance's opposition to military strikes on the Houthis in the leaked Signal chat. Republicans are less likely than Democrats to have concerns about the West Bank, Gaza, and the Palestinian question more generally, but it is possible that the next generation of Republican leaders will have more reservations about the US–Israel alliance than their predecessors, especially if the nuclear threat from Iran is perceived as having been resolved. And all of this takes place against the backdrop of a ferocious debate among conservatives about whether far-right figures accused of antisemitism, such as Nick Fuentes, have a place in their movement.

One other aspect of Middle East policy is especially important for future commitments. Near the end of its term, the Biden administration introduced the AI Diffusion Rule, which treated computing power as a scarce resource and sought to limit the export of advanced AI chips and models by creating different tiers of trusted partners. In practical terms, the Diffusion Rule would likely prevent countries such as the United Arab Emirates from hosting some of the world's most important frontier data centres for artificial intelligence. The Trump administration rescinded the Diffusion Rule and embraced the notion of frontier data centres in the Middle East.

Building what may be the world's most important complex of data centres in the United Arab Emirates – and, perhaps later, in other countries in the Middle East – means placing some of America's most critical assets in the world's most geopolitically volatile region, within range of Iranian drones and missiles. For the Gulf states, these risks only sweeten the deal. If the United States senses that its vital infrastructure is in danger, it will be more likely to rush to their defence. In this way, the data centres would offer a silicon shield for the Middle East nations, as well as grant them leverage in their relations with both America and China. Moreover, the deal threatens to pull the United States further into the region at a time when successive administrations have tried to focus on the Indo-Pacific.

AMERICA IS NOT THE ONLY ONE SHAPING WORLD ORDER

Living in Washington, DC, it can sometimes be tempting to think that the world revolves around the United States. There is no question that US foreign policy and what happens in America affects the world profoundly. But the rest of the world has agency. Other countries will assess their changing external environment and make adjustments.

Canadian prime minister Mark Carney made this clear in a speech at the World Economic Forum in Davos when he said, 'We are in the midst of a rupture [in world order], not a transition' and as a result 'the middle powers must act together, because if we're not at the table, we're on the menu.'[124]

The first reality the world needs to grapple with is that Donald Trump's return to power confirms that the era of the rules-based or liberal international order is over, at least for now. These terms were always flawed and never fully captured the nuances of world order, but there was a kernel of truth to them.

During the Cold War, they meant that the United States embedded itself in a system of rules and institutions and exercised a significant degree of restraint. After the Cold War, these terms took on additional meanings – security competition between the major powers was muted; multilateral institutions such as the International Monetary Fund and the World Trade Organization had a significant influence on state behaviour (while never fully constraining it); the world economy remained open with low tariffs; and certain norms, like that against territorial expansion, were assumed to be a permanent part of world order.

All of that has now fallen apart. The Republican Party in the United States wants to break out of the old constraints and has embraced tariffs. Many powers are willing to use force if they think they can get away with it. The norm against territorial expansion has been widely abandoned, including by the president of the United States. An arms race is underway on drones and artificial intelligence capabilities, and international institutions are being systematically sidelined. With no leader willing to organise other nations to tackle shared problems, the world will also remain particularly vulnerable to external shocks, whether a financial collapse, a pandemic, an artificial intelligence crisis, or something else.

There are still remnants of the old order. US alliances are troubled but intact; the United Nations, International Monetary Fund, and other institutions still exist, albeit with less influence than before; some international rules have stayed in place. But there is no doubt that several genies have escaped their bottles and no one knows with confidence where we go from here. Amid such uncertainty, and without a global leader helping to provide public goods, countries are likely to act unilaterally to protect their interests, even if that hurts others.

America's allies and partners are hedging by investing in their own defence, just as successive administrations have urged. In an optimistic scenario, by the end of the Trump administration, America will have more capable allies that are doing more for their own security. But that might be easier said than done. Most allies are operating under severe fiscal constraints, especially in Europe. They each have internal politics with no guarantees that they will secure enough support to pass larger defence budgets at a time when they are cutting social spending. Indeed, such a move could empower populist nationalists who are less concerned about China and Russia. And there will be a strong temptation to invest in national industry and jobs-heavy programs rather than coordinating to build a coherent regional deterrent and fund new technologies.

America's adversaries and competitors are likely to continue to deepen their alignment and cooperation. Over the past four years, we have seen dramatic developments on this front. Russia has integrated its defence industrial base with China and signed a new mutual defence treaty with North Korea, receiving troops for its war against Ukraine and vast quantities of weapons. In exchange, it has provided valuable technological and military assistance to each. Russia and China are also working closely together to build a world that is resilient to Western pressure and to organise countries to push for an alternative that is more reflective of their interests, including through the BRICS and the Shanghai Cooperation Organisation. We should expect this partnership to deepen and strengthen.

America's allies may confront significant dilemmas and choices as their ties to the United States weaken and China, Russia, and North Korea intensify their alignment and engage in a massive arms build-up. One dilemma pertains to extended deterrence, whereby the United States promises to defend allies with its nuclear weapons. There has always been a question around whether the United States would, to use the Cold War terminology, sacrifice

New York to defend Paris, but successive presidents have stood by this commitment. In recent years, South Korea has expressed concern about the reliability of the extended deterrent and its leaders have openly considered whether they should acquire their own nuclear weapons.

Thus far, the Trump administration has continued the policy of extended deterrence, but the doubts around US alliance commitments may cause allies to take a hard look at the nuclear option. Given the long lead times to prepare and build a nuclear weapons program, allies will need to have confidence that the American nuclear umbrella will continue to function for at least a decade more, if not longer. If they lack that confidence, they may seek other options. Those options are complicated. For example, if South Korea decides to acquire nuclear weapons, it could lead to an act of aggression by North Korea or to coercive diplomacy by China. It may also lead to additional proliferation, including by Japan but also Middle Eastern nations. European countries such as Germany and Poland are less likely to seek their own deterrent, but they may deepen nuclear cooperation with France and the United Kingdom.

It is clear that we are in a new era in which many of the assumptions that underpinned world politics for the past 35 years no longer apply. There are now two Americas, two visions of world order that share little in common and point in very different directions. Neither is likely to triumph over the other. The world will have to live with and respond to both.

Acknowledgements

The first week of December 2023 was a particularly busy one for me. I had just come back from a 24-hour trip to India and was supposed to go to Ukraine with the national security adviser the following week, but then President Zelenskyy told us he might come to Washington around that time. On Thursday 7 December, I stopped by the Irish ambassador's Christmas drinks event for less than an hour and then left for the short walk home to review a memo my team had prepared on whether to go ahead with our Ukraine trip.

I got to a pedestrian crossing just past the Naval Observatory in Washington, DC, at 9.38 p.m. I waited. A car stopped and I began to walk across, acknowledging the driver with a wave of my hand. Another car kept going in a second lane and struck me. A witness told the police I was thrown 20 feet in the air. I was in a coma and had two skull fractures, five facial fractures, a smashed shoulder, numerous other injuries, and bleeding on the brain.

In the days and weeks that followed, I was the beneficiary of extraordinary medical care at George Washington Hospital and of tremendous support to my family by my White House colleagues. I was incredibly blessed with a miraculous recovery and to make it back to work after a three-month absence. As I write this paper, which will be the closest I get to a memoir of my time in the Biden administration, I want to acknowledge and thank all of those who helped me at that defining moment. My colleagues were truly a very special group of people. I will be forever grateful.

I'd like to particularly thank my former colleagues Jake Sullivan, Kurt Campbell, Vidya Neelakantan, and Nate Reynolds for conversations and advice that helped with this paper. After the Biden administration, I was fortunate to return to the Brookings Institution as a Senior Fellow, which is where I wrote this. I would like to thank my colleagues Suzanne Maloney, Mike O'Hanlon, Bruce Jones, Alejandra Rocha, and Natalie Britton. Thank you too to *The Atlantic*, particularly Jeff Goldberg, Yoni Appelbaum, and Laura Secor for publishing my work, including several articles that helped me formulate the ideas I used here.

I was delighted to rejoin the Lowy Institute as a Nonresident Fellow after the White House. My good friend Michael Fullilove convinced me to write this paper and without his encouragement I probably would not have written about my time in the administration. Sam Roggeveen helped me formulate the ideas, led this project on Lowy's side, and continuously improved the paper. Clare Caldwell is an exceptional editor and was a pleasure to work with. Thank you also to two anonymous reviewers.

Above all, thank you to my wife Karen and my son Senan for putting up with lots of late-night writing and for their love and support.

Endnotes

1 Joseph R. Biden, 'Remarks by President Biden and Secretary of State Antony Blinken on the Administration's Work to Strengthen America and Lead the World', The White House National Archives, Delivered 13 January 2025, Published 15 January 2025, https://bidenwhitehouse.archives.gov/briefing-room/speeches-remarks/2025/01/15/remarks-by-president-biden-and-secretary-of-state-antony-blinken-on-the-administrations-work-to-strengthen-america-and-lead-the-world/.

2 The White House, *National Security Strategy*, October 2022, https://bidenwhitehouse.archives.gov/wp-content/uploads/2022/10/Biden-Harris-Administrations-National-Security-Strategy-10.2022.pdf.

3 John Lewis Gaddis, *Strategies of Containment: A Critical Appraisal of American National Security Policy during the Cold War*, (New York: Oxford University Press, 2005).

4 Lester W. Grau and Ali Ahmad Jalali, 'The Soviet–Afghan War: Breaking the Hammer & Sickle', *VFW Magazine*,

January 2002, https://realcontextnews.com/wp-content/uploads/2022/03/0203_Soviet-Afghan-War.pdf.

5 Pjotr Sauer, 'One Million and Counting: Russian Casualties Hit Milestone in Ukraine War', *The Guardian*, 22 June 2025, https://www.theguardian.com/world/ng-interactive/2025/jun/22/one-million-and-counting-russian-casualties-hit-milestone-in-ukraine-war; Seth G. Jones and Riley McCabe, 'Russia's Battlefield Woes in Ukraine', Center for Strategic International Studies, 3 June 2025, https://www.csis.org/analysis/russias-battlefield-woes-ukraine.

6 Gabrielle Tétrault-Farber and Tom Balmforth, 'Russia Demands NATO Roll Back from East Europe and Stay Out of Ukraine', Reuters, 18 December 2021, https://www.reuters.com/world/russia-unveils-security-guarantees-says-western-response-not-encouraging-2021-12-17/.

7 Joseph R. Biden Jr., 'President Biden: What America Will and Will Not Do in Ukraine', *The New York Times*, 31 May 2022, https://www.nytimes.com/2022/05/31/opinion/biden-ukraine-strategy.html.

8 Bob Woodward, *War*, (New York, NY: Simon & Schuster, 2024), p.150.

9 *War*, p.157; See also David Ignatius, 'The Strategist in the Hurricane', *The Washington Post*, 31 December 2024, https://www.washingtonpost.com/opinions/2024/12/31/national-security-adviser-jake-sullivan-biden-world-crisis/.

10 *War*, p.155.

11 Ignatius, 'The Strategist in the Hurricane'.

12 For example, see Christina Arabia, Andrew Bowen, and Cory Welt, *U.S. Security Assistance for Ukraine*, (Washington, DC: Congressional Research Service,

22 May 2024), https://www.congress.gov/crs-product/IF12040; Adam Entous, 'The Partnership: The Secret History of the War in Ukraine', *The New York Times*, 29 March 2025, https://www.nytimes.com/interactive/2025/03/29/world/europe/us-ukraine-military-war-wiesbaden.html.

13 David Axe, 'New Guns, More Ammo: Ukraine's Artillery Blasts Away at a Rate of Millions of Shells a Year', *Forbes*, 28 February 2025, https://www.forbes.com/sites/davidaxe/2025/02/28/as-supply-chains-come-online-ukraines-artillery-blasts-away-firing-millions-of-shells-a-year/.

14 Cédric Pietralunga, 'European-Trained Ukrainian F-16 Pilots will not be Ready Until Late 2024', *Le Monde*, 25 April 2024, https://www.lemonde.fr/en/international/article/2024/04/25/european-trained-ukrainian-f-16-pilots-will-not-be-ready-until-late-2024_6669456_4.html; Constant Méheut, 'Ukraine has Received F-16 Fighter Jets, Zelensky Says', *The New York Times*, 4 August 2024, https://www.nytimes.com/2024/08/04/world/europe/ukraine-f-16-fighter-jets.html.

15 Natasha Bertrand and Katie Bo Lillis, 'Russia Pulled Back Weapons Shipment to Houthis amid US and Saudi Pressure', CNN, 2 August 2024, https://edition.cnn.com/2024/08/02/politics/russia-weapons-houthis-saudi-arabia; Bojan Pancevski, Thomas Grove, Max Colchester, and Daniel Michaels, 'Russia Suspected of Plotting to Send Incendiary Devices on US-Bound Planes', *The Wall Street Journal*, 4 November 2024, https://www.wsj.com/world/russia-plot-us-planes-incendiary-devices-de3b8c0a.

16 Anton Troianovski and Ivan Nechepurenko, 'Putin Declares Changes to Russian Nuclear Doctrine', *The New York Times*, 25 September 2024, https://www.

nytimes.com/2024/09/25/world/europe/putin-russia-nuclear-doctrine.html.

17 Lara Jakes, 'What is Russia's Oreshnik Ballistic Missile', *The New York Times*, 27 November 2024, https://www.nytimes.com/2024/11/27/world/europe/russia-oreshnik-ballistic-missile.html.

18 David E. Sanger and Julian E. Barnes, 'US Fears Russia Might Put a Nuclear Weapon in Space', *The New York Times*, 17 February 2024, https://www.nytimes.com/2024/02/17/us/politics/russia-nuclear-weapon-space.html.

19 For an updated account of assistance to Ukraine, see 'Ukraine Support Tracker, Kiel Institute, https://www.kielinstitut.de/topics/war-against-ukraine/ukraine-support-tracker/. On South Korea artillery rounds, see Gordon Lubold and Michael R. Gordon, 'South Korean Artillery Supply Allows US to Delay Decision on Cluster Munitions for Ukraine', *The Wall Street Journal*, 24 May 2023, https://www.wsj.com/world/south-korean-artillery-supply-allows-u-s-to-delay-decision-on-cluster-munitions-for-ukraine-4e41c04b; on Israel, see Eric Schmitt, Adam Entous, Ronen Bergman, John Ismay, and Thomas Gibbons-Neff, 'Pentagon Sends US Arms Stored in Israel to Ukraine', *The New York Times*, 17 January 2023, https://www.nytimes.com/2023/01/17/us/politics/ukraine-israel-weapons.html.

20 Aamer Madhani, 'US Intelligence Finding Shows China Surging Equipment Sales to Russia to Help War Effort in Ukraine', Associated Press, 19 April 2024, https://apnews.com/article/united-states-china-russia-ukraine-war-265df843be030b7183c95b6f3afca8ec.

21 Tom Balmforth and Mariano Zafra, 'Thousands of Troops, Millions of Shells, Reuters, 15 April 2025, https://www.reuters.com/graphics/UKRAINE-CRISIS/NORTHKOREA-RUSSIA/lgvdxqjwbvo/.

22 Stella Kim and Mithil Aggarwal, 'North Korea Confirms It Sent Troops to Russia, Calling Them "Heroes"', *NBC News*, 28 April 2025, https://www.nbcnews.com/world/asia/north-korea-confirms-sent-troops-russia-calling-heroes-rcna203245.

23 Ministry of Foreign Affairs of the People's Republic of China, 'China's Position on the Political Settlement of the Ukraine Crisis', 24 February 2023, https://www.mfa.gov.cn/eng/zy/gb/202405/t20240531_11367485.html.

24 Sylvie Zhuang, 'Brazilian President Wraps up China Visit by Telling US to 'Stop Encouraging' War in Ukraine', *South China Morning Post*, 15 April 2023, https://www.scmp.com/news/china/diplomacy/article/3217202/brazilian-president-wraps-china-visit-telling-us-stop-encouraging-war-ukraine.

25 O Globo Editorial Board, '"Neutralidade" de Lula Revela Apoio Tácito à Rússia', *O Globo*, 17 April 2023, https://oglobo.globo.com/opiniao/editorial/coluna/2023/04/neutralidade-de-lula-revela-apoio-tacito-a-russia.ghtml.

26 For the July 2021 essay, see Vladimir Putin, 'On the Historical Unity of Russians and Ukrainians', President of Russia, 12 July 2021, http://en.kremlin.ru/events/president/news/66181. For an example of other utterances, see Ministry of Foreign Affairs of the Russian Federation, 'President of Russia Vladimir Putin's Speech at the Meeting with Senior Staff of the Russian Foreign Ministry', 14 June 2024, https://mid.ru/en/foreign_policy/news/1957107/. See also AFP, 'Putin Says Ukraine Peace Talks Possible, but Not with Zelensky', *The Moscow Times*, 29 January 2025, https://www.themoscowtimes.com/2025/01/29/putin-says-ukraine-peace-talks-possible-but-not-with-zelensky-a87775.

27 Helene Cooper and Edward Wong, 'Downing of Chinese Spy Balloon Ends Chapter in a Diplomatic Crisis', *The New York Times*, 4 February 2023, https://www.nytimes.com/2023/02/04/us/politics/chinese-spy-balloon-shot-down.html.

28 For example, see Kurt M. Campbell and Ely Ratner, 'The China Reckoning', *Foreign Affairs*, 13 February 2018, https://www.foreignaffairs.com/china/china-reckoning.

29 Rush Doshi, *The Long Game: China's Grand Strategy to Displace American Order*, (New York, NY: Oxford University Press, 2021).

30 For example, see Saif M. Khan, 'US Semiconductor Exports to China: Current Policies and Trends', Center for Security and Emerging Technology, October 2020, https://cset.georgetown.edu/publication/u-s-semiconductor-exports-to-china-current-policies-and-trends/; Andrew Imbrie, Ryan Fedasiuk, Catherine Aiken, Tarun Chhabra, and Husanjot Chahal, 'Agile Alliances: How the United States and Its Allies Can Deliver a Democratic Way of AI', Center for Security and Emerging Technology, February 2020, https://cset.georgetown.edu/publication/agile-alliances/; Ely Ratner, Daniel Kliman, et al., 'Rising to the China Challenge: Renewing American Competitiveness in the Indo-Pacific', Center for a New American Security, 28 January 2020, https://www.cnas.org/publications/reports/rising-to-the-china-challenge.

31 Kurt M. Campbell and Jake Sullivan, 'Competition without Catastrophe', *Foreign Affairs*, 1 August 2019, https://www.foreignaffairs.com/china/competition-with-china-catastrophe-sullivan-campbell.

32 The White House, *National Security Strategy*, October 2022, https://bidenwhitehouse.archives.gov/wp-content/uploads/2022/10/Biden-Harris-Administrations-National-Security-Strategy-10.2022.pdf.

33 Ibid.

34 Ibid.

35 Patrick Wintour, Angelique Chrisafis, and Julian Borger, 'Biden Admits to Macron the US was "Clumsy" in AUKUS Submarine Deal', *The Guardian*, 30 October 2021, https://www.theguardian.com/world/2021/oct/29/biden-admits-macron-us-was-clumsy-submarine-deal.

36 For the rationale behind the administration's approach, see Jake Sullivan, 'Remarks at the Special Competitive Studies Project Global Emerging Technologies Summit', The White House, 16 September 2022, https://bidenwhitehouse.archives.gov/briefing-room/speeches-remarks/2022/09/16/remarks-by-national-security-advisor-jake-sullivan-at-the-special-competitive-studies-project-global-emerging-technologies-summit/.

37 Brian Deese, 'The Biden White House Plan for a New US Industrial Policy', Atlantic Council, 23 June 2021, https://www.atlanticcouncil.org/commentary/transcript/the-biden-white-house-plan-for-a-new-us-industrial-policy/; Brian Deese, 'Remarks on Executing a Modern American Industrial Strategy', The White House, 13 October 2022, https://bidenwhitehouse.archives.gov/briefing-room/speeches-remarks/2022/10/13/remarks-on-executing-a-modern-american-industrial-strategy-by-nec-director-brian-deese/; Jake Sullivan, 'Remarks on Renewing American Economic Leadership at the Brookings Institution', 27 April 2023, https://bidenwhitehouse.archives.gov/briefing-room/speeches-remarks/2023/04/27/remarks-by-national-security-advisor-jake-sullivan-on-renewing-american-economic-leadership-at-the-brookings-institution/; Jake Sullivan, 'Remarks by APNSA Jake Sullivan at the Brookings Institution', 23 October 2024, https://bidenwhitehouse.archives.gov/briefing-room/speeches-remarks/2024/10/23/remarks-by-apnsa-jake-

sullivan-at-the-brookings-institution/. On the reaction to the Sullivan 2023 speech, see Emily Benson et al., 'Reactions to National Security Advisor Jake Sullivan's Brookings Speech', The Brookings Institution, 2 May 2023, https://www.brookings.edu/articles/reactions-to-national-security-advisor-jake-sullivans-brookings-speech/.

38 For an example of Katherine Tai's perspective, see 'Remarks of Ambassador Katherine Tai Outlining the Biden–Harris Administration's "Worker-Centered Trade Policy"', Office of the United States Trade Representative, 10 June 2021, https://ustr.gov/about-us/policy-offices/press-office/speeches-and-remarks/2021/june/remarks-ambassador-katherine-tai-outlining-biden-harris-administrations-worker-centered-trade-policy. See also, Katherine Tai, 'Testimony of Ambassador Katherine Tai before the Senate Finance Committee Hearing on the President's 2022 Trade Policy Agenda', Office of the United States Trade Representative, 31 March 2022, https://ustr.gov/about-us/policy-offices/press-office/speeches-and-remarks/2022/march/testimony-ambassador-katherine-tai-senate-finance-committee-hearing-presidents-2022-trade-policy.

39 Lara Jakes and Steven Lee Myers, 'Tense Talks with China Left US Officials "Cleareyed" about Beijing's Intentions Officials Say', *The New York Times*, 19 March 2021, https://www.nytimes.com/2021/03/19/world/asia/china-us-alaska.html.

40 Author's notes.

41 Kurt Campbell and Rush Doshi, 'America Alone Can't Match China, but with Our Allies, It's No Contest', *The New York Times*, 7 September 2025, https://www.nytimes.com/2025/09/07/opinion/us-trump-china-allies.html.

42 Ibid.

43 Ely Ratner, 'The Case for a Pacific Defense Pact', *Foreign Affairs*, 27 May 2025, https://www.foreignaffairs.com/china/case-pacific-defense-pact-ely-ratner.

44 Kurt M. Campbell and Jake Sullivan, 'The Case for a US Alliance with India', *Foreign Affairs*, 4 September 2025, https://www.foreignaffairs.com/united-states/india-alliance-jake-sullivan-kurt-campbell.

45 Thomas Wright, 'Donald Trump's 19th Century Foreign Policy', *Politico Magazine*, 20 January 2016, https://www.politico.com/magazine/story/2016/01/donald-trump-foreign-policy-213546/; Thomas Wright, *The 2016 Presidential Campaign and the Crisis of US Foreign Policy*, (Sydney: The Lowy Institute for International Policy, 7 October 2016), https://www.lowyinstitute.org/publications/2016-presidential-campaign-crisis-us-foreign-policy.

46 Marshall Cohen and Jamie Gangel, 'Read the Stolen Letter from Trump's Desk Reported in Bob Woodward's Book', CNN, 6 September 2018, https://www.cnn.com/2018/09/06/politics/trump-woodward-book-trade.

47 Minho Kim, 'At a News Conference, President Refuses to Rule Out Using Force to Take Greenland', *The New York Times*, 7 January 2025, https://www.nytimes.com/2025/01/07/us/politics/trump-greenland.html. On Trump's interest in McKinley, see Asma Khalid, 'Why Trump Loves Former President McKinley So Much', NPR, 3 February 2025, https://www.npr.org/2025/02/03/nx-s1-5272753/why-trump-loves-former-president-mckinley-so-much.

48 Célia Belin, Majda Ruge, and Jeremy Shapiro, 'Imagining Trump 2.0: Six Scary Policy Scenarios for a Second Term', European Council on Foreign Relations, 12 June 2024, https://ecfr.eu/publication/imagining-trump-2-0-six-scary-policy-scenarios-for-a-second-term/.

49 Donald J. Trump, 'The Inaugural Address', The White House, 20 January 2025, https://www.whitehouse.gov/remarks/2025/01/the-inaugural-address/.

50 The White House, 'Fact Sheet: President Donald J. Trump Declares National Emergency to Increase Our Competitive Edge, Protect Our Sovereignty, and Strengthen Our National and Economic Security', 2 April 2025, https://www.whitehouse.gov/fact-sheets/2025/04/fact-sheet-president-donald-j-trump-declares-national-emergency-to-increase-our-competitive-edge-protect-our-sovereignty-and-strengthen-our-national-and-economic-security/#:~:text=Fact%20Sheet%3A%20President%20Donald%20J,his%20order%20imposes%20responsive%20tariffs.

51 'President Trump's Mindless Tariffs will Cause Economic Havoc', *The Economist*, 3 April 2025, https://www.economist.com/leaders/2025/04/03/president-trumps-mindless-tariffs-will-cause-economic-havoc.

52 Donald J. Trump, 'Remarks at a Rose Garden Event', 2 April 2025, https://rollcall.com/factbase/trump/transcript/donald-trump-speech-economic-tariffs-rose-garden-april-2-2025/.

53 Tyler Pager, Maggie Haberman, Ana Swanson, and Jonathan Swan, 'From "Be Cool!" to "Getting Yippy": Inside Trump's Reversal on Tariffs', *The New York Times*, 9 April 2025, https://www.nytimes.com/2025/04/09/us/politics/trump-tariff-pause-be-cool.html.

54 Robin Wigglesworth, 'A Treasury Market Meltdown Postmortem', *Financial Times*, 10 April 2025, https://www.ft.com/content/af032e00-982c-4507-8ae7-5acbedbc1b30.

55 The Budget Lab, 'State of US Tariffs: October 30, 2025', Yale University, https://budgetlab.yale.edu/research/state-us-tariffs-october-30-2025.

56 Time Staff, 'Read the Full Transcript of Donald Trump's "100 Days" Interview with TIME', *Time Magazine*, 25 April 2025, https://time.com/7280114/donald-trump-2025-interview-transcript/.

57 Steve Miran, 'CEA Chairman Steve Miran Hudson Institute Event Remarks', The White House, 7 April 2025, https://www.whitehouse.gov/briefings-statements/2025/04/cea-chairman-steve-miran-hudson-institute-event-remarks/.

58 Adam S. Posen, 'The New Economic Geography: Who Profits in a Post-American World?', *Foreign Affairs*, 19 August 2025, https://www.foreignaffairs.com/united-states/new-economic-geography-posen.

59 The White House, *National Security Strategy*, December 2017, https://trumpwhitehouse.archives.gov/wp-content/uploads/2017/12/NSS-Final-12-18-2017-0905.pdf; Department of Defense, 'Summary of the 2018 National Defense Strategy of the United States of America', 19 January 2018, https://media.defense.gov/2020/May/18/2002302061/-1/-1/1/2018-NATIONAL-DEFENSE-STRATEGY-SUMMARY.PDF; Mike Pence, 'Remarks on the Administration's Policy towards China', Hudson Institute, 4 October 2018, https://www.hudson.org/events/1610-vice-president-mike-pence-s-remarks-on-the-administration-s-policy-towards-china102018; Mike Pompeo, 'Communist China and the Free World's Future', US Department of State, 23 July 2020, https://2017-2021.state.gov/communist-china-and-the-free-worlds-future-2/.

60 'China Tariff Escalation a Big Mistake, US Treasury Secretary Says', Reuters, 8 April 2025, https://www.reuters.com/world/us/china-tariff-escalation-big-mistake-us-treasury-secretary-says-2025-04-08/.

61 Adam S. Posen, 'Trade Wars are Easy to Lose: Beijing has Escalation Dominance in the US–China Tariff Fight', *Foreign Affairs*, 9 April 2025, https://www.foreignaffairs.com/united-states/tariffs-trade-wars-are-easy-lose.

62 Evan Halper and Jeff Stein, 'US Agencies Alarmed by China's Curbs on Exports of Rare-Earth Minerals', *The Washington Post*, 24 April 2025, https://www.washingtonpost.com/business/2025/04/24/rare-earths-trade-war-us-china/.

63 US Geological Survey, *Mineral Commodity Summaries 2022*, US Department of the Interior, 31 January 2022, https://pubs.usgs.gov/publication/mcs2022.

64 Brooke Escobar, Ammar A. Malik, Sheng Zhang, et al., *Power Playbook: Beijing's Bid to Secure Overseas Transition Minerals, Executive Summary*, AIDDATA, (Williamsburg, VA: AidData at William & Mary, 2025), https://docs.aiddata.org/reports/china-transition-minerals-2025/EXECUTIVE_SUMMARY_Power_Playbook.pdf.

65 The White House, *National Security Strategy*, November 2025, https://www.whitehouse.gov/wp-content/uploads/2025/12/2025-National-Security-Strategy.pdf.

66 Katie Bo Lillis, Alayna Treene, Kylie Atwood, and Kaitlin Collins, 'White House Fires Multiple Administration Officials after President Meets with Far-Right Activist Laura Loomer', CNN, 4 April 2025, https://www.cnn.com/2025/04/03/politics/nsc-firings-trump-laura-loomer-meeting.

67 Demetri Sevastapulo, 'US Senators Seek to Block Nvidia Sales of Advanced Chips to China', *Financial Times*, 5 December 2025, https://www.ft.com/content 0e4e4799-b340-4cee-bdbc-6a6325f77eac.

68 Bilahari Kausikan, 'Who's Afraid of America First?', *Foreign Affairs*, 7 January 2025, https://www.foreignaffairs.com/united-states/whos-afraid-america-first-bilahari-kausikan-trump.

69 Lawrence Wong, 'Ministerial Statement by PM Lawrence Wong on the US Tariffs and Implications', Prime Minister's Office, Singapore, 8 April 2025, https://www.pmo.gov.sg/Newsroom/Ministerial-Statement-by-PM-Lawrence-Wong-on-the-US-Tariffs-and-Implication; Ng Eng Hen, 'Remarks By Minister For Defence Dr Ng Eng Hen at the BMW Foundation Herbert Quandt Annual Leaders Roundtable, "On the Horns of a Trilemma: Geopolitical Recession, Technological Leadership and Energy Security"', Munich Security Conference, 14 February 2025, https://www.mindef.gov.sg/news-and-events/latest-releases/15feb25_speech.

70 Sui-Lee Wee, 'Hegseth Seeks to Reassure Allies on First Official Trip to Asia', *The New York Times,* 28 March 2025, https://www.nytimes.com/2025/03/28/world/asia/hegseth-philippines-china.html.

71 Pete Hegseth, 'Remarks by Secretary of Defense Pete Hegseth at the 2025 Shangri-La Dialogue in Singapore', US Department of War, Singapore, 31 May 2025, https://www.war.gov/News/Speeches/Speech/Article/4202494/remarks-by-secretary-of-defense-pete-hegseth-at-the-2025-shangri-la-dialogue-in/.

72 Demetri Sevastopulo, 'US Demands to Know What Allies Would Do in Event of War over Taiwan', *Financial Times*, 12 July 2025, https://www.ft.com/content/41e272e4-5b25-47ee-807c-2b57c1316fe4.

73 Ryan Neelam, *Lowy Institute Poll 2025 Key Findings Report*, 16 June 2025, https://poll.lowyinstitute.org/report/2025/executive-summary/#global-powers-and-world-leaders.

74 Kristi Govella, 'New Documents Reveal Next Steps for US–Japan Trade Deal', Center for Strategic and International Studies, 9 September 2025, https://www.csis.org/analysis/new-documents-reveal-next-steps-us-japan-trade-deal.

75 'Japan Survey Finds Only 22% of Respondents Trust US; Significant Drop From Joint Poll', *The Japan News*, 30 June 2025, https://japannews.yomiuri.co.jp/politics/politics-government/20250630-266708/.

76 Jesse Johnson, 'Japan Scraps "Two-Plus-Two" Meeting with US over Defense Spending Demand, Report Says', *The Japan Times*, 21 June 2025, https://www.japantimes.co.jp/news/2025/06/21/japan/politics/japan-us-two-plus-two-cancelled/.

77 Andrew Higgins and Javier C. Hernández, 'China's "Wolf Warrior" Diplomacy Returns with Threat against Japan's Leader', *The New York Times*, 13 November 2025, https://www.nytimes.com/2025/11/13/world/asia/china-japan-takaichi-taiwan.html.

78 Lingling Wei, Brian Schwartz, Meridith McGraw, and Jason Douglas, 'Trump, After Call With China's Xi, Told Tokyo to Lower the Volume on Taiwan', *Wall Street Journal*, November 27 2025, https://www.wsj.com/politics/national-security/trump-after-call-with-chinas-xi-told-japan-to-lower-the-volume-on-taiwan-3af795d6.

79 Kristi Govella, 'Japan's Response to Trump 2.0: Sustaining US Ties, Strengthening International Partnerships,' Center for Strategic and International Studies, October 6 2025, https://www.csis.org/analysis/japans-response-trump-20-sustaining-us-ties-strengthening-international-partnerships.

80 'South Korea Cannot Pay $350 Billion to US for Tariff Deal as Trump Suggests, Top Aide Says', Reuters, 28 September 2025, https://www.reuters.com/world/

asia-pacific/south-korea-cannot-pay-350-billion-us-tariff-deal-trump-suggests-top-aide-says-2025-09-27.

81 Raphael Rashid, 'South Korea Outraged as 300 Workers Treated as "Prisoners of War" in US Raid', *The Guardian*, 12 September 2025, https://www.theguardian.com/global-development/2025/sep/12/south-korean-outrage-at-us-detention-ordeal-as-300-workers-return-home.

82 Elbridge Colby, 'Remarks at the Sejong Institute', Seoul, 26 January 2026, https://www.war.gov/News/Speeches/Speech/Article/4389207/remarks-by-under-secretary-of-war-for-policy-elbridge-colby-at-the-sejong-insti/.

83 A. Anantha Lakshmi, 'Vietnam Risks being the Trade War's Biggest Loser. Does it have a Plan B?', *Financial Times*, 13 June 2025, https://www.ft.com/content/81caf263-7e5a-43bb-9ee4-1de1a89bc394.

84 Trevor Hunnicutt and Khanh Vu, 'Trump Says He will Put 20% Tariff on Vietnam's Exports', Reuters, 3 July 2025, https://www.reuters.com/world/asia-pacific/trump-says-he-has-struck-trade-deal-with-vietnam-2025-07-02/.

85 Yuen Foong Khong and Joseph Chinyong Liow, 'Southeast Asia is Starting to Choose', *Foreign Affairs*, 24 June 2025, https://www.foreignaffairs.com/china/southeast-asia-starting-choose-khong-liow.

86 Demetri Sevastopulo and Kathrin Hille, 'Donald Trump Blocks Taiwan's President Lai Ching-te from New York Stopover', *Financial Times*, 29 July 2025, https://www.ft.com/content/21575bec-5cdd-47ee-9db2-3031c4ea7ca7; Demetri Sevastopulo and Kathrin Hille, 'US Cancelled Military Talks with Taiwan', *Financial Times*, 30 July 2025, https://www.ft.com/content/baf4a261-1fce-4c38-b05f-ccd01d3be750.

87 Michael Martina, Yimou Lee, and Ben Blanchard, 'Trump Aims to Exceed First Term's Weapons Sales to Taiwan, Officials Say', Reuters, 30 May 2025, https://www.reuters.com/world/china/trump-aims-exceed-first-terms-weapons-sales-taiwan-officials-say-2025-05-30/.

88 Noah Robertson and Ellen Nakashima, 'Trump Nixed $400 Million in Taiwan Military Aid, Pushing Future Arms Sales', *The Washington Post*, 19 September 2025, https://www.washingtonpost.com/national-security/2025/09/18/trump-taiwan-arms-sales-military-aid/.

89 Kanishka Singh, 'US Approves Potential $330 Million Arms Sale to Taiwan, First under Trump', Reuters, 14 November 2025, https://www.reuters.com/business/aerospace-defense/us-state-dept-approves-possible-sale-taiwan-fighter-jet-spare-repair-parts-2025-11-14/; Ben Blanchard and Michael Martina, 'US Announces $11 Billion Arms Package for Taiwan, Largest Ever', Reuters, 18 December 2025, https://www.reuters.com/world/china/taiwan-says-us-has-initiated-111-billion-arms-sale-procedure-2025-12-18/.

90 David Shepardson and Steve Holland, 'Trump and TSMC Announce $100 Billion Plan to Build Five New US Factories', Reuters, 4 March 2025, https://www.reuters.com/technology/tsmc-ceo-meet-with-trump-tout-investment-plans-2025-03-03/.

91 The White House, 'United States–India Joint Leaders' Statement', 13 February 2025, https://www.whitehouse.gov/briefings-statements/2025/02/united-states-india-joint-leaders-statement/.

92 US Embassy India, 'Vice President JD Vance Remarks on the US and India's Shared Priorities,' 22 April 2025, https://in.usembassy.gov/vice-president-jd-vance-remarks-on-the-u-s-and-indias-shared-priorities/.

93 Jeff Cox, 'Treasury Secretary Bessent Says It's Up to China to De-Escalate Trade Tensions', CNBC, 28 April 2025, https://www.cnbc.com/2025/04/28/treasury-secretary-bessent-says-its-up-to-china-to-de-escalate-trade-tensions.html.

94 Anupreeta Das, Suhasini Raj, and Showkat Nanda, 'At Least 24 Tourists Gunned Down by Militants in Kashmir', *The New York Times*, 22 April 2025, https://www.nytimes.com/2025/04/22/world/asia/kashmir-terrorist-attack.html.

95 Donald J. Trump, post, *Truth Social*, 10 May 2025, https://truthsocial.com/@realDonaldTrump/posts/114483405683675564.

96 Mujib Mashal, Tyler Pager, and Anupreeta Das, 'The Nobel Prize and a Testy Phone Call: How the Trump–Modi Relationship Unraveled', *The New York Times*, 30 August 2025, https://www.nytimes.com/2025/08/30/us/politics/trump-modi-india.html.

97 Elian Peltier, 'Pakistan is in Trump's Good Graces but for How Long?', *The New York Times*, 13 August 2025, https://www.nytimes.com/2025/08/13/world/asia/pakistan-trump-munir.html.

98 Associated Press, 'Read the Full Text of Trump's Speech to a Joint Session of Congress', PBS NewsHour, 5 March 2025, https://www.pbs.org/newshour/politics/read-the-full-text-of-trumps-speech-to-a-joint-session-of-congress.

99 Rick Noack, 'Inside Pakistan's Strikingly Successful Washington Charm Offensive', *The Washington Post*, 20 September 2025, https://www.washingtonpost.com/world/2025/08/20/pakistan-trump-india-munir-oil/.

100 Michael R. Gordon, 'White House Says Pakistan is Developing Long-Range Missile Capable of Hitting the US', *The Wall Street Journal*, 23 December 2025, https://www.wsj.com/politics/national-security/white-

house-says-pakistan-is-developing-long-range-missile-capable-of-hitting-the-u-s-0863d5eb.

101 Andrew Roth, 'Trump Claims to be a "Peacemaker" as He Promises to "Take Back" the Panama Canal', *The Guardian*, 20 January 2025, https://www.theguardian.com/us-news/2025/jan/20/trump-vows-to-take-back-panama-canal-in-us-foreign-policy-vision.

102 Munich Security Conference 2025, *Speech by JD Vance and Selected Reactions, Volume II*, (Munich: Munich Security Conference, 2025), p.16, https://securityconference.org/assets/02_Dokumente/01_Publikationen/2025/Selected_Key_Speeches_Vol._II/MSC_Speeches_2025_Vol2_Ansicht_gek%C3%BCrzt.pdf.

103 Ibid., p.34.

104 'The Leaked Signal Chat, Annotated', *The New York Times*, 25 March 2025, https://www.nytimes.com/interactive/2025/03/25/us/signal-group-chat-text-annotations.html.

105 Adriana Gomez Licon, 'What They Said: Trump, Zelenskyy and Vance's Heated Argument in the Oval Office', Associated Press, 28 February 2025, https://apnews.com/article/trump-zelenskyy-vance-transcript-oval-office-80685f5727628c64065da81525f8f0cf.

106 Barak Ravid, 'Trump's "Final Offer" for Peace Requires Ukraine to Accept Russian Occupation', Axios, 22 April 2025, https://www.axios.com/2025/04/22/trump-russia-ukraine-peace-plan-crimea-donbas.

107 Gregory Svirnovskiy, 'JD Vance Says Russia has Asked for Territory it Hasn't Won', *Politico*, 8 May 2025, https://www.politico.com/news/2025/05/08/jd-vance-says-russia-has-asked-for-territory-it-hasnt-won-00337243.

108 For the Russian memo, see 'Ukraine's Neutrality, Recognition of Donbass, Novorossiya: Key Ideas of Russian Memorandum', Tass News Agency, 2 June 2025, https://tass.com/politics/1967467/amp; For the Ukrainian memo, see 'Ukrainian Proposals for June 2 Talks with Russia in Istanbul', Reuters, 1 June 2025, https://www.reuters.com/world/europe/ukrainian-proposals-june-2-talks-with-russia-istanbul-2025-06-01/.

109 Joey Garrison, '"Oh Really?": Trump Says his Wife Melania has Some Thoughts on Vladimir Putin', USA Today, 14 July 2025, https://www.usatoday.com/story/news/politics/2025/07/14/melania-trump-input-vladimir-putin-russia/85195997007/.

110 'Kremlin Says Security Guarantees for Ukraine Cannot be Provided by Foreign Military, RIA Reports', Reuters, 4 September 2025, https://www.reuters.com/world/europe/kremlin-says-security-guarantees-ukraine-cannot-be-provided-by-foreign-military-2025-09-05/.

111 April Rubin, 'Trump Says European Union is "Nastier than China"', Axios, 12 May 2025, https://www.axios.com/2025/05/12/trump-european-union-trade-war-china-tariffs.

112 'NATO Concludes Historic Summit in The Hague', North Atlantic Treaty Organization, 27 June 2025, https://www.nato.int/en/news-and-events/articles/news/2025/06/27/nato-concludes-historic-summit-in-the-hague.

113 The White House, 'Fact Sheet: The United States and European Union Reach Massive Trade Deal', 28 July 2025, https://www.whitehouse.gov/fact-sheets/2025/07/fact-sheet-the-united-states-and-european-union-reach-massive-trade-deal/.

114 See, for example, Kurt M. Campbell and Rush Doshi, 'Underestimating China', *Foreign Affairs*, 10 April 2025, https://www.foreignaffairs.com/china/underestimating-china.

115 Jessica Chen Weiss, 'The China Trap', *Foreign Affairs*, 18 August 2022, https://www.foreignaffairs.com/china/china-trap-us-foreign-policy-zero-sum-competition; Jessica Chen Weiss, 'The Case Against the China Consensus', *Foreign Affairs*, 16 September 2024, https://www.foreignaffairs.com/united-states/case-against-china-consensus; Nancy Okail and Matthew Duss, 'America is Cursed by a Foreign Policy of Nostalgia', *Foreign Affairs*, 3 December 2024, https://www.foreignaffairs.com/united-states/america-cursed-foreign-policy-nostalgia.

116 Rebecca Lissner and Mira Rapp-Hooper, 'Absent at the Creation?', *Foreign Affairs*, 24 June 2025, https://www.foreignaffairs.com/united-states/absent-creation-rebecca-lissner.

117 Elissa Slotkin, US Senator for Michigan, 'Slotkin Lays Out New Vision for American National Security, Keyed to Middle-Class Priorities', Remarks Delivered at the Council on Foreign Relations, 8 September 2025, https://www.slotkin.senate.gov/2025/09/08/icymi-slotkin-lays-out-new-vision-for-american-national-security-keyed-to-middle-class-priorities/.

118 Ian Ward, 'Is There Something More Radical Than MAGA? JD Vance is Dreaming It', *Politico*, 15 March 2024, https://www.politico.com/news/magazine/2024/03/15/mr-maga-goes-to-washington-00147054.

119 Ibid.

120 Cara McGoogan, 'In Ohio, Vance Faces Backlash in Ukrainian Community over War Stance', *The*

Washington Post, 23 October 2022, https://www.washingtonpost.com/politics/2022/10/23/vance-ukraine-war-ohio-senate/.

121 The White House, *National Security Strategy*, November 2025, https://www.whitehouse.gov/wp-content/uploads/2025/12/2025-National-Security-Strategy.pdf.

122 Lin Yang, 'Vice Presidential Nominee Vance Calls China "Biggest Threat to Our Country"', *Voice of America*, 16 July 2024, https://www.voanews.com/a/vice-presidential-nominee-vance-calls-china-biggest-threat-to-our-country-/7701298.html.

123 Barak Ravid, 'Scoop: White House Scolded Netanyahu for Violating Gaza Ceasefire with Strike', Axios, 15 December 2025, https://www.axios.com/2025/12/15/israel-violate-ceasefire-gaza-strike-trump.

124 Mark Carney, 'Davos 2026: Special Address by Mark Carney, Prime Minister of Canada', World Economic Forum, 20 January 2026, https://www.weforum.org/stories/2026/01/davos-2026-special-address-by-mark-carney-prime-minister-of-canada/.

Lowy Institute Penguin Specials

1. *Beyond the Boom*, John Edwards (2014)
2. *The Adolescent Country*, Peter Hartcher (2014)
3. *Condemned to Crisis*, Ken Ward (2015)
4. *The Embarrassed Colonialist*, Sean Dorney (2016)
5. *Fighting with America*, James Curran (2016)
6. *A Wary Embrace*, Bobo Lo (2017)
7. *Choosing Openness*, Andrew Leigh (2017)
8. *Remaking the Middle East*, Anthony Bubalo (2018)
9. *America vs The West*, Kori Schake (2018)
10. *Xi Jinping: The Backlash*, Richard McGregor (2019)
11. *Our Very Own Brexit*, Sam Roggeveen (2019)
12. *Man of Contradictions*, Ben Bland (2020)
13. *Reconstruction*, John Edwards (2021)
14. *Morrison's Mission*, Paul Kelly (2022)
15. *Rise of the Extreme Right*, Lydia Khalil (2022)
16. *Modern Warfare*, Sir Lawrence Freedman (2023)
17. *Best Laid Plans*, Sean Turnell (2024)
18. *India in a World Adrift*, Shivshankar Menon (2025)
19. *The Myth of the Asian Century*, Bilahari Kausikan (2025)

THE MYTH OF THE ASIAN CENTURY

Bilahari Kausikan

A LOWY INSTITUTE PAPER

It's time to peel away the layers of a cliché that is not just useless, but harmful.

The claim that the twenty-first century will be Asian, just as the twentieth century was American, is often made but seldom examined. Yet this axiom is not just simplistic, it could also encourage the very rivalry that most threatens Asia's security and prosperity: between the United States and China. Asia is certainly playing a more prominent role in global geopolitics, just as Europe once did and America still does. The purpose of this Paper is to unpack the many layers concealed by the phrase 'the Asian Century'. The future is too complex to be characterised by any one continent.